# TOWARD SIGNIFICANCE

A GUIDE FOR PASTORING WELL

**TENTHPOWER**PUBLISHING
www.tenthpowerpublishing.com

Copyright 2020 by David A. Davis

Scripture quotations are from the ESV® Bible (The Holy Bible, English Standard Version®), copyright © 2001 by Crossway, a publishing ministry of Good News Publishers. Used by permission. All rights reserved.

Scriptures taken from the Holy Bible, New International Version®, NIV®. Copyright © 1973, 1978, 1984, 2011 by Biblica, Inc.™ Used by permission of Zondervan. All rights reserved worldwide. www.zondervan.com The "NIV" and "New International Version" are trademarks registered in the United States Patent and Trademark Office by Biblica, Inc.™

Design by Inkwell Creative

Softcover ISBN: 978-1-938840-37-1
e-book ISBN: 978-1-938840-38-8

10 9 8 7 6 5 4 3 2 1

Pastor David Davis invites readers to understand the significance of ministry while also providing practical ways to navigate each element of ministry. This book is a must read for pastors and those who support them.

—Andrew Bauer, Executive Pastor of Team Development
  Blythefield Hills Baptist Church
  Rockford, Michigan

Dave Davis has written a book that will serve pastors (and the elders' leaders who love them) well. From a pastor with enough road miles to give him the credibility, he writes as a trusted guide and offers helpful and hopeful counsel and reflections that will both encourage and gently guide pastors regardless of where they are in their ministry. The journey from success to significance is crucial for all of us as we live into all that God has in store for us. Pastor Davis' book is a wonderful resource to accompany pastors as they seek to ensure significant, sustainable, and joyful ministry for the long haul.

—Scott Bolinder, Executive Director
  Institute for Bible Reading

I have known Dave Davis for more than twenty years. He is wise, witty and pithy. Whenever I have a conversation with him, I leave with a smile on my face and a new insight in my head. His new book is like a series of those conversations. His insights on character, habit and organization will leave you smiling and lead you into a clear understanding of what it takes to have a ministry of significance in today's Church.

—Greg Finke, Executive Director, Dwelling 1:14
  Author, *Joining Jesus on His Mission*

Pastor Davis offers the pithy, practical, unvarnished advice of a seasoned pastor who wisely puts first "He [Jesus] must increase and I must decrease." Most will find themselves nodding along at points, laughing, and perhaps disagreeing, too. Regardless, it's good for pastors to think on how best to serve the flock the Lord has entrusted to our loving and committed distribution of His gifts.

—David C. Fleming, Executive Director for Spiritual Care
  DOXOLOGY: The Lutheran Center for Spiritual Care and Counsel

As a life-long church member, former elder, and retired seminary professor, I warmly recommend this wise and edifying book by Rev. David Davis. It shares the reflections and insights of a seasoned pastor who has incorporated and effectively applied his seminary education to decades of congregational ministry. The first chapter elaborates the basic theme of the book—that significant ministry is a divine calling that glorifies Christ, proclaims the Gospel, reaches the lost, and promotes love within and beyond the congregation. A dozen subsequent chapters focus on important qualities, responsibilities, practices, and pitfalls in the life and work of a pastor. Each chapter is based on a relevant passage of Scripture, candidly focuses on an essential aspect of a pastor's life and ministry, offers sound practical advice, and concludes with questions for discussion. At first glance what Davis writes might seem like common sense. But on reflection, it is uncommon sense—biblical wisdom—given the influence of self-fulfillment, pastors' personalities, entertainment, and marketing on much current ministry.

Davis' book is accessible and engaging—more like lively sermons than an instruction manual. Although primarily for ministers and elders, it will benefit whole congregations. Church members should be aware of and appreciate the gifts, responsibilities, and challenges of their pastors. But they also share their pastors' calling to follow Christ, and much of this book is about glorifying Christ and growing in his likeness. I commend *Toward Significance* to a wide Christian readership. Davis is a faithful LCMS minister, but what he writes will bless all who affirm Holy Scripture, historic Christian orthodoxy, and the Gospel of salvation for everlasting life through Jesus Christ.

—John W. Cooper, Ph.D., Professor of Philosophical Theology Emeritus
  Calvin Theological Seminary

Reading through Dave's sage counsel reminded me of the first time I laid eyes on C. H. Spurgeon's Morning & Evening. The practical and insightful wisdom he shares will serve the church for generations to come. There are few things as beneficial and refreshing as sitting at the feet of someone who has learned masterful lessons over the course of a lifetime, and then allowing the character of that person to speak into your life. Such is the gracious gift which Dave has provided to the body of Christ. *Toward Significance* is like a long cool drink of water on a hot July day.

—Mark Kring, Sr. Pastor
  New Hope, a biblical community
  Haslett, Michigan

Dave Davis has been an acquaintance of mine for a number of years. He's been a friend for the past few years. And now I've discovered that he's even more intelligent than I ever realized. How so? When he asked if I would provide an endorsement for the book you're about to read, I agreed, thinking I'd say a few generic words and be done with my promise. But then I actually read what he had written. Wow! This is good stuff! Practical, I like that. Systematic, I respect that. Spiritual, I'm blessed by that. Christocentric, I'm super blessed by that. It's also helpful, especially for young pastors, I'm thankful for that. Actually, I think if I had been aware of all the stuff in this book earlier in my ministerial career, I might have achieved something of greater significance in life and ministry. Read this book. You'll be glad you did!

—Rev. Dr. Gerald B. (Jerry) Kieschnick, President Emeritus
 The Lutheran Church—Missouri Synod

Rev. David A. Davis has dealt with one of the most important attributes a pastor should learn very early in ministry, that is, the mission of serving God's people is about glorifying Jesus as preeminent, Lord and Savior; preaching the Gospel, which is the power of salvation for all humanity; reaching the lost souls for the kingdom of God; growing Christians in love, the great commandment and decreasing daily as Christ increases in the mission and ministry of His Church on earth. This book is a much-needed pastoral care resource manual for pastors and elders for the purpose of understanding the true significance of the work of Christ, His Church and called servants in order to serve God's people in growing a healthy, faith-filled, Christ-centered communion of saints. Rev. David Davis' book interprets his experience of many years of pastoral concern, care, compassion and compulsion for the communion of saints he has served over the years. May his years of ministry attributes help the reader to gain needed insight in serving Christ in their Witness, Mercy, Life Together—In Christ, for the Church and the World.

—Rev. Dr. Roosevelt Gray, Jr., Pastoral Ministry Director,
 Black and African Ministry
 Office of National Mission, The Lutheran Church—Missouri Synod

Wisdom, practical wisdom. I am always on the hunt for what is logical, real, practical and true. If you care about ministry, if you care about your ministry, this is a valuable book that can help you avoid the ditches others have fallen into. Significant ministry depends on it.

—Jeff Schrank, Pastor
  Christ Lutheran Church
  Best Practices Ministry Conference
  Phoenix, Arizona

This book is engaging—for the mind and the heart; it's insightful—with questions, answers, and many examples of "I should have known that"; and inspiring—for ministry, family life, relationships and personal excellence. I've known Pastor Davis for more than three decades and have greatly appreciated him as a mentor, sounding board, and am thankful to count him a close friend. His passion for Jesus and the Good News and truth has always been evident in his life. His desire for Jesus' lost ones to be found as a blessed responsibility for all—clergy and laity—shines. But it's his care for pastors and ministries—that they be vibrant, joyous, life-sustaining and giving—which predominates.

Wisdom lived, learned, and gathered from decades of reading and experience can be mined and discovered in this book. What he writes, he believes, he lives, and he has done. For example, he has read through the Bible every year for the decades I've known him. What does this mean? (Good Lutheran question.) It means that the Holy Spirit has spent time with him... molding, shaping, and gifting generous amounts of wisdom and grace.

And now this: a gem of a book that compels us into a similar relationship with God; a book that should be read by pastors and church leaders together, at seminaries as men prepare for the highest of callings, by pastors together, or simply by men's groups ... for as "Iron sharpens iron, so one man sharpens another" Proverbs 27:17. It's a primer for a godly, humble, righteous significance.

—David P.E. Maier, President, Michigan District
  The Lutheran Church—Missouri Synod

*Toward Significance* is a great resource opportunity offered to you from a seasoned mentor. Pastor Davis doesn't dismiss striving to make your congregation flourish but does put pastoral leadership in its proper place, a consequence of your own humble, Savior-centered trust in the God who makes us sufficient for ministry. "We also believe and so we also speak" (2 Corinthians 4:13). Here's hoping that many pastors, young and also experienced, will use and share this personally edifying and ministry enhancing resource!

—Rev. Dr. Dale A. Meyer, President (Retired)
Concordia Seminary
St. Louis, Missouri

Pastors need pruning or they become larger than life. Here is a book for pastors unwilling to leave behind the little things and the real people that Jesus has entrusted to their care. This is a handbook, practical and indispensable. Each section offers the pastor a glimpse of his own sermons and emails and temptations with a view toward what is accounted significant in God's Word. Like the Ten Commandments, the fundamentals of good pastoring do not change and it is perilous to move beyond them. Here are the everyday principles for working and dwelling in the congregation and not above it.

—Steven Newberg, Pastor
Ascension Lutheran Church
Charlotte, North Carolina
*Recipient of original essays that comprise this book*

Certain wisdom comes only from the school of maturity, while engaging the everyday curriculum of trial-and-error, within a classroom of experiential refinement. Especially during these times of crisis and seeming insanity, David Davis' words ground us. I was refreshed by his workable fidelity, practical integrity, and the ordinary examples of how to demonstrate toward others the love with which we, by Christ Jesus, were first loved. All readers will delight in Davis' witty ways of unfurling that uncommonest of virtues, common sense; but Christian leaders, in particular, will find usable tools in this accessible collection to let their lights shine to God's glory.

—John Arthur Nunes, Ph.D., President
Concordia College-New York

As a fledgling pastor just learning the ropes of ministry, I was aided greatly by regular letters of experience-born wisdom from Pastor Dave Davis, letters that became the seedbed of this book. His letters greatly sharpened me toward what was good, right, and meaningful in ministry and steered me away from many of the common snares the Enemy sets for servants of God. No doubt, this book will do the same for all who read it. This volume will benefit the novice pastor attempting to chart a faithful course of ministry. It will also benefit all pastors in reevaluating and recalibrating ministry and life in order to recapture what is most important. It's been eleven years of ministry since I first read the letters that compose this book. They all still ring true and are invaluable. Davis' words will help you grow a significant ministry and life.

—Ted Torreson, Pastor
 The Exchange Community
 East Jackson, Missouri
 *Recipient of original essays that comprise this book*

In this refreshing and readable book, Dave Davis writes with wit and wisdom that are instantly recognizable to those who know and love him. Here is a collection of essays aimed at helping church leaders find and produce significance in Kingdom work. Far from being a doctrinal slog, *Toward Significance* offers practical advice that turns out to be deeply theological. Wondering if Dave's advice is pertinent to the challenges that pastors face, I came to the realization that what he writes is applicable to everyone who loves Jesus. Maybe if I practiced what he preaches, my pastor's job would be easier. Bravo to Dave for resisting the temptation to add pages of unnecessary verbiage to add gravitas to the topic. He writes what needs to be said in a personal and accessible style and moves on. Underpinning all of these wonderful essays is the core question, "Is Jesus being glorified?" Yes!

—John P. Varineau, Associate Conductor, Grand Rapids Symphony
 Professor of Music (retired), Calvin University

Pastor Dave Davis has shaped my ministry—and my life!—with his wisdom, insights, and encouragement. *Toward Significance* captures the best of his ministry wisdom and makes it available to all who read this book. Whether you are beginning your first years of ministry, approaching your final years, or looking to support the work of your congregation, this book must be on your reading list.

—A. Trevor Sutton, Associate Pastor
St. Luke Lutheran Church
Haslett and Lansing, Michigan
Author, *Being Lutheran; Clearly Christian;* and *Why Should I Trust the Bible?*

Sometimes you respect someone because they always agree with you. But, I fear that is a form of self-love. Sometimes you respect someone because they challenge you. They may have differences in approach, or style, or whatever. But, you walk away from your interactions knowing that you've met someone with intelligence, competence, integrity, zeal, and a sense of mission that you hope others see in you. This is the respect and Christian love I have for Pastor Dave Davis. I've been privileged to serve with him in The Lutheran Church—Missouri Synod for years. I've been privileged to see the wonderful fruit that his parenting skills have borne. I've rejoiced at the hospitality of his table. I rejoice that some of the saints I love have gotten to know him as a friend and shepherd under Christ. I can tell you that when he writes a book, you should be sure to read it. He will challenge, inform, and uplift you. Best of all, you will hear God's Word from a skilled pastor.

—Rev. Robert Zagore, Executive Director
Office of National Mission
The Lutheran Church—Missouri Synod

# TOWARD SIGNIFICANCE

A GUIDE FOR PASTORING WELL

DAVID A. DAVIS

TENTH POWER

## WITH THANKS

I am thankful for the women in my life who have loved me and guided my life and ministry toward greater significance. They have made me a better person and given me a clearer picture of what significance in life and ministry actually are. When I went looking for success, they pointed me *toward significance*. I give thanks to God for my wife, Sallie, who likes "the Jesus sermons" best, our four daughters, Laura, Anna, Caroline, Ellen, my widowed (now-sainted) mother, Anne, my sisters Elizabeth and Margaret, and recently—and joyfully—our two grand-daughters Gemma and Clara.

# TABLE OF CONTENTS

About the Author  19
Foreword  21
Introduction  25

CHAPTER ONE: Sine Qua Non  29
*1 Timothy 3:1-17*
Our Significance in Ministry
On Reading through the Bible
On Prayer
On Tithing

CHAPTER TWO: Work Is Work  43
*John 9:1-7*
On Hard Work
On Working Hard
On Reverence and Irreverence
On a Silver Bullet

CHAPTER THREE: Tricks of the Trade  55
*Proverbs 14:15-18*
On Selective Neglect
On Outlines
On Latin
On Turning Things Upside Down

CHAPTER FOUR: Disciplines of the Person  69
*1 Timothy 4:6-9*
On Diet and Exercise
On Fasting
On Memorization of Scripture
On Drinking

CHAPTER FIVE: Pastoral Habits  79
*James 3:1-11*
On Talking about Members
On Listening
On Words to Watch
On Recognition

CHAPTER SIX: Household Helpers  91
*Ephesians 5:25-33; Luke 14:25-33*
On Family Time
On Holidays
On Being a Home-Going Pastor
On the Long Haul

CHAPTER SEVEN: Big Three Plus One  105
*1 Corinthians 10:1-13; Matthew 20:20-28*
On Money
On Sex
On Power
On Truth-Telling

CHAPTER EIGHT: Professional Duties   119
*Deuteronomy 17:14-20*
On Leadership
On Preaching
On Meetings
On Public Prayer

CHAPTER NINE: A Life's Endeavor   133
*Proverbs 6:9-11*
On Reading
On Book Clubs
On New and Old Things
On Excelling

CHAPTER TEN: In the Flesh   145
*1 Samuel 16:1-13*
On Smiling
On Manners
On Shoes
On Clerical Garb

CHAPTER ELEVEN: Life Out There   155
*Acts 17:16-34*
On Meeting the Needs of the Community
On Sports
On Straightening Pictures
On Playing the Hand You Are Dealt

CHAPTER TWELVE: Warning  **169**
*Ephesians 6:10-20*
On Joy
On Discouragement
On Boundaries
On War

CHAPTER THIRTEEN: Embrace the Adventure  **183**
*Psalm 1*
On Juggling
On Tinkering
On Your Pastoral Example
On Pastoral Perspective

# ABOUT THE AUTHOR

God backed me into being a pastor. It was not my first choice. It was not on my radar.

When asked, "When did you know you wanted to be a pastor?" I have come to answer, "About fifteen years into it." For those first many years I kept thinking there has to be something else I can do... anything else.

But when God calls...

I am grateful for the privilege of being a parish pastor now for over 35 years. It has been a calling of *significance*. My ministry has not been written up in *Christianity Today*; I was never listed on the twenty-five new Christian leaders to watch; my congregation was never the fastest growing in the county... but there has always been *significance*. People have come to know Jesus. Marriages have been healed. Young people have been guided toward discipleship. Leaders have been developed.

Read the Bible. Spend more time in prayer. Serve. Preach the Gospel, with words—engaging and quirky. See what's the most you can do. This has been my approach to ministry and *significance*.

Long ago I read Chuck Colson who wrote that only two things can save America: the family and the local congregation. My dedicated path *toward significance* has been:

- Love, serve and be faithful to my family

- Give myself over to the health of the local congregation—mine and others.

Come join me in a quest for something more than success. Let's experience significance!

—Rev. David A. Davis

# FOREWORD

This book is about "significance in ministry." "Significance in ministry" lifts up Christ, proclaims the good news, reaches out to the lost, and shows love toward others. "Significance in ministry" also sums up the theme of conversations that all pastors can benefit from. I realize this last sentence may come across as a platitude, but I say it because I first got to know Dave Davis in just such a conversation.

Like the sons of many pastors, I wanted to be a pastor. Until I was seven. Nearly twenty years passed before I again thought about the ministry.

When I began to reconsider, my father assumed the responsibility of making sure I knew what I might be getting myself into. Right away, he made me arrange to spend a few days with him. I don't actually remember much about them, except that we went on some calls, and then he explained why he prayed early in his visits and how he used hymn verses with the dying; except that he gave detailed reasons for how to arrange, schedule, and organize meetings; except his arguments for not giving children's sermons and for not blessing children at the communion rail; except… Okay: I remember more than I thought.

But I need to add one more memory: visiting with Dave Davis.

Dave was in the first few years of pastoral ministry. He would meet regularly with my father, who was at a neighboring congregation. During that visit with my father, I joined them for breakfast. I don't remember what they talked about, mostly because I didn't understand what they talked about.

The point, however, was not that I understood the conversation, but that I would value that they were talking and, even more, appreciate Dave's outlook. My father didn't come out and say this, probably under the principle that it would be better caught than taught. But I think I caught it. In fact, this book shows me that I know I caught it.

What was that outlook? I don't know how Dave would have answered at the time, but the answer of this book would have made as much sense then as it does now: "He must increase, and I must decrease."

No pastor would disagree, but the real question is "How?" Here you might be tempted to say, "You have to work it out for yourself." Each pastor needs to have his own answer to "How?" But you don't learn to think for yourself; you learn to think with others.

Alan Jacobs made this point in his helpful book *How to Think* by recounting the story of Megan Phelps-Roper. In case you do not know about her, she is a granddaughter of Fred Phelps, the long-time pastor of Westboro Baptist Church in Kansas. Phelps and members of the church have been infamous for their demonstrations against homosexuals and dead military personnel. Megan Phelps-Roper was deeply involved from her youth, and as a young adult, she took the lead with their social media. She encountered a lot of hateful and vile reactions, but she also came across someone genuinely interested in why she believed what she believed. And she started to think about that. When she realized that she might have been wrong about one thing, she understood that she might have been wrong about many things. So she thought more about her beliefs, her life, herself. In time, she left the demonstrations, the church, and her family.

Jacobs imagines that most people would conclude that Megan Phelps-Roper had finally stopped blindly accepting what others told her and learned to think for herself. But Jacobs keenly points out that thinking for yourself is impossible. What really happened was that she learned to think with others.

As a young pastor Dave may not have understood explicitly that you learn to think with others, but he clearly acted that way. This was so clear that my father thought it important that I meet Dave when I was just beginning to consider the ministry.

This book demonstrates Dave has not changed in this regard. To be sure, he is in a different place now. He is the one whom others might ask for a half-hour to talk or ask out for breakfast. But he knows and values thinking with others.

Thinking in itself is not necessarily a good thing, but thinking and rethinking how Christ might increase and we decrease are good things. The thirteen chapters range all over the place. The topics run from preaching and praying to selective neglect to occasional use of Latin to having enough time for sex (don't worry—that is as far as he goes). Undoubtedly you will find some things obvious, some things wrongheaded, some things irrelevant, some things needed. But drawing such conclusions isn't all that this book is about. Talking and thinking with others are more to the point.

So, as you read the book, argue with the author, or discuss it with another pastor, or use it with fellow Christians. Use the questions, and think of some more questions yourself. And together, confirm what you do know about significance in ministry, and think of fresh ways by which Christ be lifted up, the good news proclaimed, the lost reached, and love shown to all.

—Joel P. Okamoto, Th.D.
Waldemar and Mary Griesbach Professor of Systematic Theology
Chair, Department of Systematic Theology
Concordia Seminary

# INTRODUCTION

This book will cure you of "steeple envy"—or least will reduce its symptoms. Not every pastor will pastor a mega-church. Statistically, most won't.

But the size of the congregation does not directly correlate with the significance of a pastor's ministry. Significance in ministry will result as a consequence of fixing peoples' eyes on Jesus, God's great sign of love. (Hebrews 12:2) Significance in ministry is more about… *significance*… than it is about numbers of members.

- Is Jesus being glorified?
- Is the Gospel being preached?
- Is the lost world being reached?
- Are Christians growing in love for each other and their community?
- Or, in the spirit of John the Baptist, is Christ increasing, and are we decreasing?

These are issues of significance, and attention to them will lead you to it.

The following topics will help pastors of "normal-size congregations" grow in greater significance in ministry. They do not focus on theology or doctrine as such. You will find no theological axe-grinding. Rather they will help you consider issues of character, habit, and organization. Such topics, properly managed, will help you avoid stumbling blocks, increase the significance of your ministry, and inoculate you against steeple envy.

This collection grows out of what started as fifty-two essays written for a couple of young men who had grown up in my congregation. The idea was to give them a dose of encouragement and direction once a week for their first year of ministry. Since I first wrote these essays, I have shared them with dozens of first-year pastors over the course of the last decade.

In this book I have re-designed them to be considered and discussed in community. I recommend that pastors engage their elders or other leaders to join in the study of this book. To that end, each chapter includes a brief conversation guide.

Ultimately, pastoral ministry transcends the building of steeples or, for that matter, large multi-purpose family-life centers. Rather it invites a pastor on an adventure of eternal significance where he decreases and Christ increases. May this book lead you toward that… *significance*!

## WHAT IS "SIGNIFICANCE"?
### DEFINING (OR AT LEAST EXPLAINING) MY TERM

Like so many other English words *significance* stems from a Latin word. The Latin root means to indicate or to portend. You can easily see the word "sign" within it. A sign, for instance a stop sign, stands in for and bears the message of another. It indicates another's message. Instead of having a policeman at the corner telling people that they must stop before proceeding, a stop sign is placed with that message. The sign delivers a message on behalf of another.

In that sense a pastor, or any Christian for that matter,

is to be a sign for Another. We are ambassadors of Christ. By definition, at least in this root form of the word, pastoral ministry serves to indicate Another and his Gospel message. To grow *toward significance* means that we grow in more clearly bearing the message of Jesus; we are a sign for him.

In English the main meaning of the word "significance" is *the quality of being important.*

Congregational ministry generally and pastoral ministry specifically have the quality of being important. Read most any popular critical assessment\* of "what's wrong with things today", and you will find some conclusion about the importance of healthy Christian congregations in local communities.

Pastors and our congregations need to embrace the idea that our work is of importance. We by God's grace handle an eternal Gospel that makes an eternal difference in people's lives. Having a clear understanding of the significance of our work, we will be motivated to work on honing and enhancing our character, habit and organization. Such effort will move us *toward significance.*

The word significance gets applied in a specialized sense in regard to statistics. We hear about "statistical significance." This means that one statistic or data point or number rises above (or below) another in a way that makes a difference, in a way that ought to be noted or noticed.

This too should be on our radar. Each pastor should so steward the gifts received from God that he gets noticed. We do not want to hide our lamps under a bushel basket but make sure that our light shines for all around us. As stated later in the book, this being noticed is not about being the *best in the world* but being the *best for the world*. Pastors and congregations should orient our ministries *toward significance*, toward getting them noted or noticed, not as an end in itself, but because of the One for whom we serve as a sign.

So, let us work *toward significance* while it is day until night comes and no man can work.

\* *Our Kids*, by Robert Putnam; *Hillbilly Elegy*, by J.D. Vance; *How Now Shall We Live?*, by Chuck Colson; *Helping without Hurting*, by Steve Corbett and Brian Fikkert; *Alienated America*, by Timothy Carney.

CHAPTER ONE

# SINE QUA NON

*T*hat's a Latin phrase that means "without (this thing), (that thing) is impossible." Literally, "without which, not." Later in this book I have a section on the pastor and Latin. Latin is helpful, but not necessary. You can certainly be a pastor without even a rudimentary knowledge of Latin.

This first chapter explores, however, four topics without which it will be impossible to be a pastor with a significant ministry impact. Latin and any other number of things are helpful but not necessary. What follows is more than helpful—it is necessary.

---

## ON SIGNIFICANCE IN MINISTRY

*"He must increase, and I must decrease."* (John 3:30) John the Baptizer said it best and with the fewest words (not a bad lesson on sermons!).

Easy to say; hard to do.

As a pastor you will always struggle to tame your ego. Weekly, people will greet you warmly at the end of services and assure you that you are doing a great job, that you are a blessing to many, a real treasure from God. Watch it.

Home bound visits will end with people saying that you made their day. Watch it.

Little children will think you are Jesus. Catechism students will quote you in their public-school classes as the Voice of God. Young people will look up to you and tell you what a big difference you have made in their lives. Watch it.

Few other occupations garner the kind of regular and positive feedback that parish pastors receive. It can be so encouraging. It can also be disastrous… if you believe everything people say about you.

John Schmidt was a swell guy. That's not his name; I do not remember what it really was, but I do remember the event with great clarity. He was an older gentleman at my vicarage church who not only was always positive and encouraging, "never a discouraging word," like the old cowboy song goes, but he also always sat in the front row.

During one of my stellar vicar sermons, the only kind vicars preach, John slept. He did not doze. He did not nod off. He slept—right there in front of me! He made no pretense of trying to stay awake. The lights were off, and no one was home. Whatever was going through his mind, it had lots more to do with visions of sugar plums than it did with any theological insight coming from me.

As he left service that day, I half expected a chagrined, "Sorry about that, Vicar. We were out late last night." I mean, he was sound asleep—right there under my nose. Instead I got this, "Vicar Davis, what a wonderful sermon!"

You've got to be kidding me! He had not heard a word I said.

Now here's the scary part. *I believed him.* There was no reason to believe him, except he said what my ego always wants to hear. I believed that it was a wonderful sermon and that I was a wonderful preacher. Nothing but good things ahead for a guy like me! Sure, it was clear to me that he had not heard a word of the sermon, but I heard his word of affirmation… and used it to massage my ego. Insidious. Dangerous. Be careful. *"He must increase, and I must decrease."* Significance in ministry occurs only as Christ increases.

There are two wonderful, and related, Bible passages that can serve to keep a pastor's ego in check. Always remember Balaam, or better yet, his donkey. When your ego starts to get out of check, when *you* start to increase instead of *Jesus*, remember that you are a vessel only, and if God tires of using you, he can find any old donkey and do the same thing.

Remember the other donkey too—the Palm Sunday donkey. Jesus sent his disciples into the village to secure that donkey with the words, "The Lord has need of it." (Matthew 21:3) The thing that was special that day about the donkey was not the donkey, but the Christ he carried. That's you, fellow pastor, and me. We could just as easily be donkeys carrying Christ to people. It is not about us. It is about Jesus.

This is not to denigrate the encouragement you will receive. You will receive it, and you will need it. The Office of the Public Ministry is hard, hard work. But do not let the encouragement elevate you above Jesus.

Write it down. Say it often. Burn it into your heart. The keystone to significance in ministry is this: *"He must increase, and I must decrease."*

## ON READING THROUGH THE BIBLE

If you desire great significance in pastoral ministry, I can offer, and you can find, no better advice than the following:

This year read through the entire Bible.

When you are done, repeat the same (at least) once every year for the rest of your life... on earth. No other single activity will enhance your ministry more than this. You will not find anything closer to a silver bullet.

The following are *good* reasons not to read through the Bible at least annually:
1.
2.
3.

Okay, I can't think of one.

By *reading through the Bible* I do not mean *studying the Bible*. Certainly, you should examine in greater detail certain smaller passages of the Bible. *Studying the Bible* and *reading through the Bible* are different but not altogether separate exercises. Nor do I mean your "professional" *reading the Bible* for sermon or Bible study preparation. Certainly, preparation for preaching and teaching duties should be deeply bathed in *reading the Bible*. Professional *reading the Bible* and *reading through the Bible* are again different but not altogether separate exercises.

Reading through the Bible is to read the Bible from the front cover through to the back cover—every word.

I know that the Pharisees made Scripture their stock in trade; they were known for knowing the Scripture inside and out. Don't worry that aggressive Bible reading will turn you into a Pharisee. The problem with the Pharisees was not their discipline but their hearts. Remember, *abusus non tollit usum*! (Loosely: the misuse of something does not nullify the proper use.)

In an interview with a potential staff member I asked, "What does it mean to have a passion for Jesus?" The answer I wanted was something like "working really, *really hard* in service to him"—passion in the sense of *willingness to suffer*. His answer was better, "*To be passionate for Jesus is to be passionate about his word, for that's where he is found.*"

I like that.

Do we *believe* that the Word of God is Jesus? "And the Word became flesh and dwelt among us." (John 1:14)

Do we *believe* that to have a life and ministry centered in Jesus is to have a life and ministry centered in the Word because the Word centers in Jesus?

Do we *believe* that the Word of God is the sword of the Spirit? "Take the helmet of salvation and the sword of the Spirit, which is the word of God." (Ephesians 6:17) What in the world would ever convince us to go out into the world unarmed? What soldier goes to battle without his weapon? A doomed one!

Do we *believe* that the Word of God is light for our path? "Your word is a lamp for my feet and a light for my path." (Psalm 119:105) If the Word is light, why would we stumble through our ministry in the dark? Only foolish spelunkers leave their flashlights on a shelf when they go exploring caves.

Do we *believe* that the Word of God gives us life in a way that is even greater than that life sustained by air, water and nourishment? "These are written that you may believe that Jesus is the Christ, the Son of God, and that by believing you may have life in his name." (John 20:31) You wouldn't last too many weeks without food. You'd last only days without water and minutes without air. Not only would you grow weak without air, water and nourishment, you'd grow dead! If the Word provides greater things than these, what would ever keep us from reading at least a little bit of the Bible every single day?

Do we *believe* that the Bible is the Word *of God*? Cover to cover?

I do.

And here's the thing—in just twenty to thirty minutes a day you can read it from beginning to end in a year. Your faith, life, marriage and ministry will never be the same. There is no silver bullet to guarantee significance in ministry, but this comes close.

There are tons of plans and editions you can follow. Some plans split the Bible into four daily readings: Old Testament, Epistle, Gospel and Psalm. There is one edition out there that has cut and pasted the entire Bible into chronological order. A friend of mine uses what I'll call the *Mehren's Method*: (Step 1) find the page number on the last page of the Bible, (Step 2) write that number down, (step 3) divide that number by 365, then (Step 4) read that many pages daily… this method has to be adjusted during leap year.

Experiment with different translations through the years.

This is a good time to brush up on (or off) your Greek. One year read all the Gospel passages in Greek. The next year try the Epistles. Or throw caution to the wind and read all the New Testament in Greek.

Overachievers can add some Hebrew.

Do not let me put this on you as a burden. Rather let me *capture your imagination*. What will ministry be like long term if as a pastor you determine to read through the entire Bible every year your entire ministry? If you are in your mid-twenties, do you think having read through the Bible fifteen times will make you more effective in your forties than you are right now? And what impact will having read through the Bible thirty-five times have on your ministry in your sixties?

In preparing this material I found a quote by Luther that suggested *twice* a year.

## ON PRAYER

Pray a lot.

Prayer is one of the great responsibilities of a pastor, publicly and privately. It is one of the "roll up your sleeves" duties. It is not a mere formality to start and end a day, a meeting or a meal.

God gave great promises about prayer.

Ask and it will be given to you; seek and you will find; knock and the door will be opened to you. For everyone who asks receives; he who seeks finds; and to him who knocks, the door will be opened. Which of you, if his son asks for bread, will give him a stone? Or if he asks for a fish, will give him a snake? If you, then, though you are evil, know how to give good gifts to your children, how much more will your Father in heaven give good gifts to those who ask him! (Matthew 7:7-11)

Martin Luther made some of the boldest statements about prayer that I have ever read. He hardly sounded "Lutheran"! Dig out a copy of the *Book of Concord* and read the introduction to the Lord's Prayer in the "Large Catechism." See the amazing things Luther said about the power of prayer and its impact on the success of the Reformation.

So… *pray aggressively*. They say Martin Luther prayed for two to three hours a day; John Calvin prayed even more. A wise pastor once counseled his pre-marriage couples that if they are too busy for sex, they are too busy! And so it is with prayer: if a pastor is too busy for prayer, he is too busy!

How much is enough? Wrong question! Paul says, "Pray without ceasing." (1 Thessalonians 5:17) Pastors should develop their prayer lives in a way that makes prayer the default setting in their lives. Unfortunately, this passage from Paul is sometimes construed in a way that works against prayer. Some say that *praying without ceasing* means that everything a Christian does is covered with prayer by virtue of his being a Christian—so that a Christian doesn't *really* need to pray. Nonsense.

The following practices will help you *pray without ceasing*:

- *Intentionally devote one-half hour to prayer each day.* This is not an ending point; it is the starting point. This will get you in a rhythm, not simply done with a duty. A friend of mine once said you don't really start praying until you have been at it for ten minutes.

- *Learn to pray on your knees.* The Church moves forward on its knees. Remember, Christians are not dualists; we are "incarnationalists." We believe that the body is a gift, although a broken one, from God and that it matters. So our body as well as our spirit needs to be involved in prayer. There is no more humbled, and therefore powerful, position for prayer than on your knees with head bowed. (You might try praying standing with your arms lifted up to the Lord. You might try praying prostrate as well.)

- *Never let a meeting at your church or a visit at the hospital happen without prayer.* Generally, the prayer will be the most effective part of the interchange. When someone comes into your office, never let that person get away without prayer. This will surprise some, comfort others and disarm not a few.

- *Find extended time for fasting and prayer on a regular basis.* I have often wondered what Jesus experienced according to his human nature when he went off to pray through the night. Try it.
- *Keep in mind that spending time in prayer is never wasting your congregation's time.* In fact, your members expect you will be praying for them! And they will be grateful for it.
- *Avoid prayerful sentiments.* Never say, "I'll pray for you," unless you will. Never say, "You've been in my prayers," unless the person has. Prayerful sentiments are irrelevant at best and deceptive at worse.
- *Keep a prayer list.* I keep mine in my head. There is probably a better place.

Remember, when we pray, *Someone is* on the other end.

Pray a lot.

A significant prayer life will speed you toward significance in ministry.

## ON TITHING

*Tithe on the gross to your local congregation. You cannot buy better financial advice than this.*

Money grips us in its hold more than we know. As a pastor you probably won't be rich, but you don't have to be rich to worship money. Financial status does not drive the worship of money. Sometimes, in fact, poor people worship money more than the rich. They are downcast without it and envious of those who have it.

Here's an easy way to determine if you or your congregation is worshipping money: *do you think more money will solve your problems?* Do you lie awake at night worrying about your congregation's financial situation? Will you go to any means to raise money in your church, as long as it "works"? Do you rest easy when the balance sheet is positive and well-heeled people are in your new member class? Remember what Luther said about the first commandment? "We should fear, love and trust in God *above all things.*" To the degree that we worry about money, do somersaults for it or rest easy because of it, we have traded in the true God for a false one.

You must come to terms with money if you are going to lead a ministry of significance. Jesus said, "You cannot serve both God and money." (Matthew 6:24) Clearly you will serve one of them!

Keep in mind that money is not the enemy of God; Satan is. Money is the *opposite* of God. God creates. Money secures creation. Money is "liquid creation."

As God's enemy, Satan schemes to get people, *especially God's people*, to put their trust and confidence in the creation instead of the Creator. Satan wants us to buy the lie that money provides security, health, peace and even love.

Nonsense.

That's where tithing helps. Tithing does two things. First, it *breaks your trust in money.* By tithing you are voluntarily giving *lots* of money away, *more than you can afford.* To the world it looks like a sailor on a sinking ship throwing away his life vest. Tithing kicks the false god in the shins: "You think I need you? You think I'm living for you? Watch, I'll give you away."

Second, tithing *forces you to trust in the true God. You cannot afford to tithe. You are a pastor!* You don't get paid much as it is. If anyone can't afford to live on less, you can't. For you to get by on just 90% of your income will take… an act of God. Oh, that's the point. Your only hope to get by on what's left of your income is the very power and love and generosity of God. Tithing forces *us* out of the way so that *God* can really be God in our lives.

And guess what? He can handle the job. God really is able to do far more than you ask or imagine. He is God. He loves to give to his children. And you cannot out give him.

Tithing calls us not just *to believe in God*, but *to believe God*. Tithing puts money in its place: servant, not master.

Additionally, the practice of tithing provides at least four side benefits. First, you won't be so awed by wealthy congregants. They will not have a disproportionate influence on you because you won't be so impressed by money. Pastors should never show partiality, especially not to the rich.

Second, you will be better able to assess your congregation from a stewardship standpoint. Your interest won't be how much money people contribute, but rather whether or not your flock increasingly trusts God. A big dollar contribution will mean nothing. Percentage of income giving will be the key.*

Third, you will learn to manage better the rest of your money. *Good financial management begins with tithing and does not exist without it.*

Fourth, you will grow in generosity. Tithing is not an ending but a beginning. Through tithing you will learn to share freely what you have with others.

Notice something I did not mention? I did not mention that tithing really increases the cash flow at church. It will. And it is the only Biblical model for doing so. We are not encouraged to sell candy or wash cars. Please leave that for the boy scouts and the marching bands to do. We should not beg, shame or cajole people into giving to meet the needs of the congregation as if our God is a needy God. Let other religions and organizations do that. Regularly modeling and teaching tithing will in fact provide for plenty in the Lord's ministry—but this is a by-product and not the motivation.

One more point. Many reject tithing as an Old Testament issue. People say it is law-oriented and never specifically encouraged in the New Testament.** I remember reading a long time ago a commentator who called it a "varnished Jewish practice."

Nonsense.

Jesus said, "Woe to you, teachers of the law and Pharisees, you hypocrites! You give a tenth of your spices—mint, dill and cummin. But you have neglected the more important matters of the law—justice, mercy and faithfulness. You should have practiced the latter, without neglecting the former." (Matthew 23:23) Clearly Jesus assumed and taught, following the practice of Abraham's pre-Covenant tithe to Melchizedek, that God's people would thankfully offer up a tithe to God.

You may think that the length of this section belies too great *a love for money*. "Why so much time thinking about tithing and money?" Just the opposite is the case. Its length argues for the crucial importance of *breaking that very love*.

So… when you get your next paycheck, before you celebrate with a dinner out or contribute to a retirement fund or make a payment on a student loan, "bring the whole tithe into the storehouse. Test the LORD in this and see if he does not open the floodgates of heaven and pour out blessings!" (Malachi 3:10)

---

\* *Note: Pastors should be informed at least in a general way what individual congregants give. You don't have to do this often. Just a few* *times in your entire ministry may suffice to give you an idea of what is really happening in your congregation when it comes to trust in God. To be ignorant of the actual giving patterns of God's people makes as much sense as having no idea who comes to church and how often.*

\*\* *Note: Never in the New Testament is the baptism of babies specifically endorsed, but the Church has long since maintained this practice.*

### Conversation: Sine Qua Non

BIBLE CONVERSATION:

Read 1 Timothy 3:1-7. How does this passage support the importance of the four concepts from this chapter?

FOR PERSONAL REFLECTION:

- How do you define *significance* in ministry?

- What if your practice of Bible reading and prayer were the practice of the entire congregation?

- Jesus said, "You cannot serve God and money." (Matthew 6:24) How can you tell which one you are serving?

FOR GROUP DISCUSSION:

- What would it look like if Jesus were "increasing" in and through your congregation? Does it look like that?

- What would it take to enhance your congregation's practice of reading through the Bible and growing in the discipline of prayer? How does pastoral leadership affect this?

- Discuss this statement: Giving motivated by meeting the needs of the congregation will perpetuate a needy congregation. How might tithing help avoid this?

GOING FORWARD:

- Identify one area of concentration for the pastor.

- Identify one area of concentration for the elders or other leadership group.

PRAYER POINTS FOR THE COMING MONTH:

CHAPTER TWO

# WORK IS WORK

Being called by God to be a pastor is a great gift. But such a call does not invite you out of the human race or into some kind of "superhumanity." To build a ministry of significance you must understand that there is nothing particularly more significant about you and your work in and of itself as opposed to any other member of your congregation. Indeed, God works his work through the Gospel and does not exempt you out of doing your work like every other human being. What is basic to everyone else's work is basic to yours too.

This chapter will help you explore four very basic concepts about how to approach your work. Work is furthered both by sustained effort and sanctified character. The best work aims for both effectiveness and efficiency.

---

## ON HARD WORK

I don't know for sure because I have never had another one, but a pastor's job looks to be one of the hardest jobs there is. So far as I have observed, the only tougher one may be that of a homemaker.

At first it amused me when people would say to me, "Boy, I would not want your job." And then it concerned me. Did I get in the wrong line somewhere?!?

This provides no excuse for a pity party or for a point of pride.

Call it reality.

You will be tested and challenged as a pastor. Don't kid yourself. The rigors are great.

*You will be challenged spiritually.* Satan and a host of evil assemble against your work. And the weaknesses of your sinful nature won't be of much help either. The temptations will not end: pride, sloth, lust, greed, gluttony, wrath and envy. Back when disco was king they said, "This ain't no disco! This ain't no foolin' around." No, it is an incredible spiritual challenge.

*You will be challenged intellectually.* You have to think through Biblical statements and apply them in multiple, contemporary situations: sermons, counseling sessions, classrooms, evangelism calls, hospital calls, staff meetings, governing board meetings, chance meetings, dinners, golf outings, et al. You must deal with people lots smarter than you. You will also deal with people far less educated than you. How do you apply what you know about what you know while considering what you don't know about what you don't know, all in a meaningful and appropriate way? What does history teach? How do your church's Confessions apply? Does science or anthropology speak to the issue? Hymnal, no hymnal, screens, printed, memorized, extemporized, old liturgy, new liturgy, what's a liturgy?

My head hurts.

So will yours.

*You will be challenged "familially."* Long ago a neighbor encouraged me to become a pastor only if I did not get married and have a family. No, he wasn't Catholic. He understood that the life of a pastor's family is a tough one. He hit the nail on the head. It's a challenge to be husband and dad at home, pastor at church, and still be the same person. It's tough for a family not to really have a pastor since the guy at home also serves as the pastor at church. It's tough for the wife to be the wife of a guy who happens to be a pastor and at the same time resist the urge or apparent necessity of serving as assistant pastor or the secretary to the pastor or the conduit to the pastor. And how does she handle hearing the "Word of the Lord" from the same fella who can't pick up his socks or get the faucet fixed? How does the husband/father/pastor balance multiple responsibilities all at once at 7:00 p.m. on a Tuesday night when a committee is meeting and the lawn needs mowing and the high school orchestra is playing and the sun is shining for the first time in a month?

*You will be challenged physically.* It's physically demanding to lead and preach two or three or four services on a Sunday. You'll be surprised. It wears you out to get up early on a Thursday for a Bible class, work all day and have a meeting that night. There is no such thing as a three-day weekend for recuperation because our weekends include Sunday! Ever visit someone who smells of feces and vomit? Ever visit with someone who has bolts screwed into her head, right into the skull, because her neck has been fused in place? You will. It takes its toll physically. Much of our work has to be done when others are either not yet fired up (Sunday mornings) or are shutting down (evening meetings)—and we need to be "on."

*You will be challenged financially.* Unless I miss my guess, no matter how much money you make as a pastor, you could find a more lucrative job that would satisfactorily match your gift set. You are going to have to set the pace in giving. The demands and schedule of your work may prohibit or limit your wife's outside employment. And again, unless I miss my guess, your congregation will always be scraping by because it has not learned to tithe. There won't be finances enough for proper staffing or continuing education. Many well-meaning members will suggest financial solutions and plans for your congregation that you need to graciously resist because they run counter to Biblical teachings. Scripture says much about money; the world says more. And you'll have to sort out which message comes from which.

*You will be challenged...* no wait, that's enough. I've made my point.

Eyes wide open. It's hard work. Don't kid yourself.

Indeed, there is much joy and fulfillment in your work. Indeed, God will bless and work all things together for your good, the good of your family and the good of the Kingdom. Indeed, God has called you to a high and noble Calling.

But it is hard work. Moving toward significance always is.

There, you are warned. Don't whine. Don't be a cry baby. Keep your head down and your feet moving.

## ON WORKING HARD

As stated before, being a pastor is hard work. Wise men approach *hard work* by *working hard*. Also as stated before, if you are looking for a forty-hour a week job that can be left at the office each evening, you should look for something else.

Through the years I have attended many "church growth" conferences and read plenty of literature on the topic. Speakers spout tons of tips on what you can do to make your congregation grow. But having watched churches that grow and churches that don't, I have observed two underreported factors:

- The work of the Holy Spirit (more on that elsewhere)
- The work of the pastor

*Pastors of growing churches are pastors who flat out work hard.*

Now working hard does not necessarily mean a seventy-hour work week, although you should be prepared for one every once in a while. It does mean being all in when you are in. Be careful about diddling your time away checking messages, chit chatting, reading the paper, traversing the internet and so on. You have things to do. You are being paid to do them. You gave your word you would do them. Do them. Do them well. *Focus; drive the work forward.*

This takes personal motivation and discipline. Working hard does not mean doing everything perfectly. In fact, part of working hard is figuring out what can be left for later or left undone. Everyone will assume you are busy and working hard, so you can get away with being a slacker… for a while. Both the perfectionist and the lazy man can find refuge in the ministry. Be neither. *Focus; drive the work forward.*

Keep in mind that you are working a work that has eternal consequences. Keep in mind that you have a Supervisor who always watches and is always present to lend a hand—and his hands are strong enough to handle anything at hand. Keep in mind that others in your congregation are at their jobs working hard, too. *Focus; drive the work forward.*

And one thing more, like two sides of scissors, combine working hard with working smart, and you'll cut through the toughest of tasks. *Focus; drive the work forward.* Drive the work toward significance.

## ON REVERENCE AND IRREVERENCE

We live in a casual culture. Men leave hats on when they enter buildings. People who formerly would have been greeted with, "Hello Mr. and Mrs. So and So," are now greeted with, "Hey Guys. 'Sup?" Hugging is done everywhere by everyone—no matter how casual or new the relationship. (Pre-COVID-19)

I do not see a cure for casualness. It is what we have become. Nor is it necessarily bad. Who would be in favor of the alternatives of stodginess or stiffness?

As pastor there is a bigger issue to contemplate: do I live a life of *reverence* or *irreverence?* This is different from whether or not I am casual. I can be stiff and still irreverent; I can be casual and still reverent.

One of the things that pastors have to watch is too great of desire to fit in, to be "with it," to be in the now. That somewhat narcissistic drive can leave *casual* behind and run head long into *irreverence*… which for a pastor is a kissing cousin ultimately to *irrelevance.*

Think *reverence.* Reverence consists of the right mixture of fear, awe, piety, devotion, respect. Reverence grows out of the reality that God really is God, here, now, wow!

*Think reverence in your language.*

James teaches about the untamable nature of the mouth. He warns that the same mouth should not utter praises and curses. See James 3:1-12.

Take that to heart. Watch what you say and how you say it. Keep in mind that while your every word is not spoken in the chancel, your every word is spoken in the presence of God and as a child of God. Your words can be casual. You can use colloquialisms. But vulgarities? No. Crassness? No. Mockeries? No, not those either.

While "thee" and "thou," "sitteth" and "standeth" are not necessary to be reverent in speech, what is necessary is an awareness that every word out of your mouth is not only a reflection of your heart but also an act of power to draw or repel people. Careful.

And while we are on the subject, as a reflection of God being a God of order, do your very best to follow proper grammar. (Although do not necessarily use my writings as a guide!) While you might use slang on occasion and for a particular effect, out of reverence for the God who has ordered all things well by his word, seek to reflect him with well-ordered words.

*Think reverence in your attire.*

I will nibble on this in subsequent chapters about shoes, clerical collars and robes. But for now, remember whom you represent: the most spectacular entity/being/reality/power.

Recently I saw a sign that is found almost nowhere these days: *proper attire required.* It was outside a fancy restaurant. The message is of course that you are about to enter into a special place (our restaurant) for a special experience (eat our fine food). Enter with awe. Enter with a little fear. Enter even with some devotion. This place will wow you. *Proper attire required.*

Wherever you are God is. And you are his. You are a child of the Most High. You represent a king, The King. *Proper attire required.*

To be reverent does not always require a tie, but sometimes it does. I have seen some pastors almost revel in their freedom to "dress down," especially in worship settings. The question is never "can we dress this way"; it is "should we". My attire, casual, formal or otherwise should always make clear to others that I am a child of the Most High God and in full devotion to him, that I am in awe.

*Think reverence in your behavior.*

Are you a crosser? Are you a bower? Some pastors cross themselves wherever they go. Some bow here, there and everywhere. Crossing and bowing at appropriate times are appropriate acts of reverence.

So are standing when others come into a room, taking your hat off indoors and keeping bodily gasses to yourself. In fact, most manners can really be construed as manifestations of reverence to God and our fellow creatures.

By the same token laughter and the joke telling that occasions it can be an act of reverence. So can listening to a great piece of music—if you understand reverence properly, there is no real distinction between sacred and secular music—accompanied by tapping your feet and clapping your hands. Our God is a God of joy. Not to give way to joyfulness is ultimately an act of… irreverence!

In your work, liturgical, official, familial, relational and casual, always keep in mind whose you are and whom you are representing. That will guide your actions toward reverence and help you avoid irreverence.

Remember, as a pastor in the Lord's church you are called *Reverend*. Seek to live up to it… even on casual Fridays. It will help your ministry's significance.

## ON A SILVER BULLET

There isn't one. At least I never found one, and I have looked hard.

Go to the conferences, read the books, attend lectures, pray for insights, but don't expect to find one silver bullet that will change everything in your ministry and provide amazing fruitfulness.

There is not one thing out there to be found that if found will give you instant success.

There are generally two kinds of instant success stories:

- Those that are a fraud built on smoke and mirrors that will ultimately tumble, and
- Those that show anything but an "instant" success. (In his book "Good to Great" James Collins describes this as what he calls a flywheel effect. Enough of the right things done over a long period of time will slowly build momentum until things seem to just take off—an "instant" success that has taken years to accomplish.)

There *is* one other kind of instant success story. Sometimes God puts his hand on someone for his purpose and grants it. It is God's doing, his gift. You can't force it. That is a rare experience.

Successful ministry and a life well-lived are a combination of lots of right, small things done well over a long period of time. That's the well-worn path toward significance.

Instead of looking for a silver bullet to propel your ministry into a book-worthy realm, keep steady focus on the following.

- Proclaim Jesus joyfully.
- Read God's word persistently.
- Pray aggressively.
- Live faithfully.
- Love impartially.
- Tinker relentlessly. (More on this later)

So, put away the fancy Lone Ranger outfit and don the ranch-hand duds. There is no silver bullet.

## Conversation: Work is Work

BIBLE CONVERSATION:

Read John 9:1-7. How does this passage support the urgency and the importance of your work as work?

FOR PERSONAL REFLECTION:

- What part of ministry do you find to be the hardest work? What part of ministry do you find to be the easiest work?

- How hard do you work when you are working? (See Ecclesiastes 9:10.)

- How do people around you know that you are working for the Most High God?

FOR GROUP DISCUSSION:

- In what way do leaders specifically, and the congregation generally, embrace the concept that the work of a local congregation is a crucial *work*?

- In what ways is the congregation's ministry rightly reverent?

- What support does the pastor need for working hard and working smart?

GOING FORWARD:

- Identify one area of concentration for the pastor.

- Identify one area of concentration for the elders or other leadership group.

PRAYER POINTS FOR THE COMING MONTH:

CHAPTER THREE

# TRICKS OF THE TRADE

*I*n any trade there are some tricks that make the work go easier and look better. I was doing a little wood working shortly after we had moved into a house. My wife thought that some wood trim around a couple rooms would dress the place up. I was having trouble making the corners come out just right. At about that time I happened, if anything ever just happens, to make a homebound visit with a retired carpenter. Having explained my plight, he showed me how to carve out the back end of one of the corner pieces so that the other one fit just right. The end result was a corner that was easier and better. Tricks of the trade.

There are any number of tricks of the trade that make the work of a pastor easier and better. These are not things you were ready to learn in seminary; you had plenty of other things to learn there. These are not the same as short cuts. This chapter explores four tricks of the trade that will help significantly.

## ON SELECTIVE NEGLECT

This chapter follows both logically and necessarily the discussions on work.

Use this tool carefully. But use it. Sometimes good enough is. Sometimes you must let *some* things go.

You cannot attend every meeting. You cannot make every visit that could be made. You cannot read every book or journal. You cannot do it all.

You cannot.

You are a pastor in the Lord's Church. You are not the Lord.

So you have to decide what you can let go *until later*. You have to decide what you can let go for *someone else to do*. You have to decide what you can *just let go*.

You have heard it said, "Do not put off until tomorrow what you can do today." That often holds true, but not always. Sometimes *you should* put off until tomorrow what you can. In "A Contrarian's Guide to Leadership," Steven B. Sample argues that a good leader at times *intentionally* puts things off until tomorrow. Some things do work themselves out without our attention. That's part of the beauty of *selective neglect*.

Of course, some things do not work out over time; they fester. So you have to *select* what to *neglect* and what not to. Choose carefully. *Selective neglect* should be used as a tool for more effective ministry, not as an excuse for sloth. And it should be used when it moves you toward significance.

Here are some tips to consider for the successful application of *selective neglect*:

- *Check your motives.* Don't be driven by your need for personal affirmation; rather be driven by what really needs to be done. For example, do you visit that person in the hospital because it makes you feel good about being a pastor or because that person really needs to see a pastor? Frankly, too much of what we pastors do is driven by our need for such affirmation rather than true ministry needs.

- *Focus on the important not the urgent.* Put off responding to some emails so that you can do quality work on your sermon. Pastors can get so caught up responding to all the little urgencies of the day that they never get to the important points of ministry.

- *Prioritize according to duty: God, family, congregation, self.* Note: balancing the God and self part is harder than the family and congregation. Think of *selective neglect* in terms of *whom* you are neglecting and not just *what*. You will choose more wisely this way.

- *Plan every day for more than a day.* Look ahead not only for the day, but also the week, month and year. Planning helps you select not only what can be neglected, but for how long. Some things can be neglected this week but must be taken care of next week.

Give the day your best shot; do what must be done. Get after it; get after it good. If there are things that can and should wait, apply *selective neglect*—wisely and carefully. Richard Swenson in "The Overload Syndrome" points out that any quitting time is an artificial distinction. There is *always* something more that can be done. But there are also things that can wait. Let them.

Remember God is in all of this! Your work doesn't ultimately depend on you. God works in and through you… and others. Part of *selective neglect* is really *trust in God*.

Every pastor should carry *selective neglect* in his bag of clubs. Make sure you do too, and use it. Carefully.

---

## ON OUTLINES

INTRODUCTION: To consistently communicate well, think in outlines. Proper application of this principle should have-wide ranging application in your ministry. The skill you learned back in fourth grade will carry you through your ministry. Outlines force better organization and sharper points. Outline everything.

I. *History*: I first came across this "outlining insight" in a little book entitled *It Takes So Little to Be above Average* by Florence Littaur. As a pastor you are going to talk… a lot. If you think in outlines, your talking will turn into communicating.

II. *Key Area*: Sermons certainly need to be well outlined. Give your listeners a better chance of understanding your message by having a reasonable progression to your presentation. Make sure you have a point and have all that you say support, elaborate and drive home that point. Words lose their punch if not married to a proper outline.

III. *Practical Examples*:

   A. *Phone calls should be outlined*. Pastors make many phone calls. Make the most of them by outlining them in advance in your head:

INTRODUCTION: Hey, good morning. How are you doing? Enjoying the weather? I have three quick things I am calling about.

1. I need help at this Friday's family night. Would you work the registration booth?
2. I wanted also to thank you for the comment you made in Bible class yesterday. Good point.
3. Don't forget that Jimmy needs to get measured for his confirmation robe at class this week.

CONCLUSION: Hope all goes well for your family this week and that Marsha gets over her cold soon. (Use the same format if you leave a voice mail.)

B. *Announcements at potlucks go better when outlined.*

INTRODUCTION: Good evening and welcome everyone. Hope you all found a seat.

1. We are going to serve table by table starting from the front left to the

   back right. Marion will dismiss each table.
2. Let's bow our heads in prayer.
3. Before we start, let's have a show of appreciation for all the good cooks and the set-up crew.

CONCLUSION: Clap warmly and encourage others to do so as well.

C. *Emails pack more punch when outlined.*

INTRODUCTION: Jim. Hope your day is going well.

1. Don't forget the meeting tonight.

2. Remember, you were going to bring that report.
3. The Ladies' Guild will have a representative there.

CONCLUSION: The meeting shouldn't last long. —Pastor D.

IV. *General Practice*: Whenever you are asked to speak, even off the cuff for a couple minutes, take a breath, collect your thoughts and put together a little outline. You'll be surprised at how much this helps. And your listeners will be surprised at what a good communicator you are even in the little things.

CONCLUSION: You do not need to write out the outline visibly with Roman Numerals for your audience. If you apply this skill properly, they will see it in their own minds. Making sure your communication of any kind is well-organized will increase the significance of your ministry.

## ON LATIN

As a pastor you should have a wide range of interests. Some new. Some old. A smattering of lots of things will provide a treasure trove for ministry. One of the things that you should have a smattering of is Latin.

There is nothing like a Latin phrase to help sell a point and to suggest significance. Lay people appreciate a well-spoken and appropriately placed Latinism. Occasionally.

Somehow a Latin phrase works better than anything in Hebrew or Greek. Seminary training accents, for obvious reasons, developing a working knowledge of Hebrew and Greek, but it is Latin that sells. Leave your Greek and Hebrew to your sermonic work.

Maybe the Biblical languages sound too foreign. We almost never see anything publicly in Hebrew, although here and there you will pick up a Yiddish phrase. The only Greek references we have in common culture are the names of sororities, fraternities and a few cities (Philadelphia, Arcadia, Attica, Clio, Marathon).

But Latin is around. Every school kid knows, "*Semper ubi, sub ubi.*" Most state mottos are in Latin. We see it on old public buildings. We use *etc., et al. and ex officio*: all from Latin. Ancient hymns and liturgical pieces keep Latin around: Gloria Patri, Nunc Dimittis, Magnificat, etc. Latin has enough of an air of familiarity that, when spoken, it makes an impact.

Now even if you never formally studied Latin, through the course of your seminary studies and with an ongoing study of theological works (which should be studied on an ongoing basis even after the seminary), you should be able to have a number of Latinisms at the ready.

Here are some of my favorites:

*Simul iustus (justus) et peccator: at the same time sinner and saint.* This description of the Christian life can be used to wiggle out of lots of those "why" questions. Why did that church treasurer abscond with the money? Why did the Sunday School teacher curse out the six-year olds? Why did we see our pastor at the pub last Friday with a third beer? (Yes, people do count.)

*Abusus non tollet usum: the misuse of something does not nullify the proper use of it.* This explains why it is still helpful to use a catechism in instructing young people even if your pastor bored you to tears with it when you were a kid.

*Cur alii, alii non: Why some and not others?* Throughout your ministry you will be faced with the perplexing work of grace. Why did this guy get saved and not that one? This phrase makes the reality no less perplexing, but it gives it a much more philosophical ring and reminds us of many who went before us and wrestled with the same question.

*Articulus stantis et (vel) cadentis ecclesiae*: The article by which the Church stands or falls. Of course, this is the doctrine of justification by grace. Indeed, without the Gospel there is no Church. But it sure sounds more significant in the Latin!

*Reformata sed semper reformanda*: Reformed and always reforming. You will find this ever true of the Church. Like a white fence that never stays so without tending, no matter what correcting has already taken place in the Church previously, there will always be plenty for you to work on and work out as a pastor. (Simile borrowed from G. K. Chesterton.)

*Hoc est corpus meum*: This is my body. You may be able to catch catechism students' attention for a bit when you explain the origin of the phrase "hocus pocus"—which, of course, is a bastardization of hoc est corpus meum.

*Oratio, meditatio, tentatio faciunt theologum*: Prayer, study and struggle make the theologian. This will be your life.

Latin helps with vocabulary. Latin helps with history. Latin helps with grammar. Latin helps with thinking. Latin helps us link with the past and the democracy of the dead. (Thanks again G. K. Chesterton.)

And at least a smattering of it will help you have a more significant ministry.

## ON TURNING THINGS UPSIDE DOWN

Somewhere, somehow you have gotten stuck as a pastor—or will. Maybe you could never quite get the sermon you were working on to come together. Maybe there is a project that hasn't quite gotten off the ground. Maybe you have not quite hit a stride in a particular area of ministry.

*Try turning things upside down.*

For instance, you may have a three-point outline that is not quite working.

I. Blue—point about something

II. Red—point about something else

III. Green—point about still something else

Try inverting the order of your points and see if the progression of your thought works better upside down.

I. Green

II. Red

III. Blue

*Try turning things upside down.*

Maybe you have a project that is slow in gaining support from others. Make sure that your first step matches theirs and that your next steps are in sync. Perhaps someone has the order wrong.

Early on I became convinced that the congregation I was serving needed a gymnasium and a classroom wing—in that order. I worked long and hard to gain support, buy-in and approval. No matter what I did resistance remained. Nothing budged.

Then we turned it upside down—not the building, but the order. "Let's go for the classroom building first and then the gym." The congregation broke ground for a new classroom building not long after that.

*Try turning things upside down.*

Perhaps your day is not as effective as you would like. No matter how hard you try, it feels like you are doing ministry with sand bags tied to your ankles.

Invert your schedule. Save what happens first in the day until the end. Move what you do at the end to the morning. Many people waste the best and most effective part of the morning by checking emails. Save them for late in the afternoon. Move your sermon prep from the afternoon, when the caffeine level drops, to the morning when you are at your sharpest. If you are a "morning person," experiment with being a "night owl" and vice versa.

*Try turning things upside down.*

Careful on this one: maybe turn the Sunday service upside down. Of course, you cannot turn the Invocation and the Benediction around, but you could move Holy Communion much earlier and move the sermon toward the end of the service. Perhaps some Sunday Holy Communion serves as the crucial spiritual food to prepare people to hear the sermon. Or start with the Gospel reading, then the New Testament reading and *then* the Old Testament reading. Reversing the order may bring particular Old Testament readings into clearer focus.

Careful on this one, too: maybe the counseling situation is the opposite of what you think. Consider the situation from the other way around. Help the counselees turn the situation upside down, and see if there is an insight they have been missing. Maybe the problem did not start "way back when"; maybe it is really a recent one. Perhaps the presenting problem is the result and not the cause of the situation.

And very careful on this one: if you have a particularly disruptive confirmation student, resist at all costs the urge to turn him upside down! But having said that, if you experience tough sledding with a class, consider the order of events in the class period and turn them around from time to time. If it does not keep the students fresh, it will at least keep them guessing, which will help them to stay engaged.

*Try turning things upside down.*

I painted a room for my granddad one summer. I had already done quite a bit of painting through the years, but I knew he had done more. So, I asked his advice as I surveyed the project, "Grandpa, how would you get started on this room?"

He said, "Well, I would start by putting the ceiling on the floor and painting it there." He spoke more wisdom than I realized.

Don't forget it was the practice of Jesus. The first will be last. (Matthew 20:16) To be great you must serve. (Mark 10:43) Those who humble themselves will be exalted. (Matthew 23:12) Whoever loses his life will find it. (Matthew 10:39)

You cannot turn every project upside down, but sometimes you can. It may prove more significant than you would guess.

*Try turning things upside down.*

## Conversation: Tricks of the Trade

**BIBLE CONVERSATION:**

Read Proverbs 14:15-18. How does this passage support the importance of the four sections just completed?

**FOR PERSONAL REFLECTION:**

- Make a list of things you accomplished this last week and things you did not accomplish. Now mark them as "important" or "urgent." How might selective neglect have made your week more significant?

- Write out an outline for an upcoming or recent phone call, email or church announcement. Experiment with turning it upside down.

- What tricks of the trade have you found in your work to make you more efficient and effective?

**FOR GROUP DISCUSSION:**

- Discuss (gently!) how clear the pastor is in communication. Are there tricks that would help him?

- Do you agree or disagree that snippets of Latin help build significance in communication? What (else) do you think helps?

- What tricks of the trade do you think would help the pastor and leaders to be more efficient and effective?

GOING FORWARD:

- Identify one area of concentration for the pastor.

- Identify one area of concentration for the elders or other leadership group.

PRAYER POINTS FOR THE COMING MONTH:

CHAPTER FOUR

# DISCIPLINES OF PERSON

Your ministry calls you to be concerned about others and their well-being. You will counsel others on marriage. You will teach others about scripture and Godly living. You will visit people who are sick and in need. You will console others in the midst of grief and loss. Pastoral ministry must be other-centered.

But to serve others well you must give attention to self-care. If you do not take care of your own body, mind and spirit you will have difficulty caring well for others. The following four topics are great places to start* to make sure that you are practicing appropriate self-care. Disciplining yourself to care for yourself will help build a ministry of significance.

*And here are a couple other resources I have found helpful for continuation in that quest. Richard Foster, "Celebration of Discipline." Dallas Willard, "The Spirit of the Disciplines."

## ON DIET AND EXERCISE

The life of a parish pastor is busy. It is a lot of things, but it is *not* a forty hour a week thing.

When we are busy, two things suffer: diet and exercise.

*Watch your diet.*

Jesus said it is not what goes into our mouth that makes us unclean, but what comes out of our mouth that makes us unclean. True enough… since Jesus said it… but what goes into our mouth can make us unhealthy and overweight!

In America, in particular, we must watch it. Food is everywhere. It is hard to imagine another place in the world or another place in history where people could so easily consume so much food that there would be entire industries dedicated to helping overweight people: diet book industry, weight loss clinic industry, stomach staple industry.

Food? Go easy on it. Portion size control is critical. Americans should down-size everything.

Watch pre-packaged foods. *Most have high levels of salt, fat and sugar.*

Watch restaurants. *See above.*

Watch snacking. *See above.*

Watch watching lots of TV. TV watching leads to snacking or going to restaurants or eating pre-packaged foods. *See above.*

Watch getting overly tired. Being overly tired leads to TV watching which leads to snacking or going to restaurants or eating pre-packaged foods. *See above.*

A variety of homemade meals in reasonable portions will almost always be all the diet strategy you will need for a healthy diet. Use your head before you use your mouth. This is excellent advice both in regard to speaking and eating.

One thing more: a practice of fasting for spiritual discipline (more on that next) will also help you to be set free from over-eating.

*Watch your exercise.*

I never scored a touchdown in high school. I never ever dunked a basketball. The one time I had a chance to score a goal in a real soccer game I choked. And golf continues to be a mystery to me.

But I walk. I do some jogging. I can even somehow tolerate using a treadmill in the basement watching cable sports.

I have no idea what works for you, but you must find something. Pastors should stay in shape.

Exercise cannot guarantee a long life; however, it will guarantee a better and more significant life in the meantime. Serving as a pastor demands physical stamina and endurance—more than most people realize. A proper exercise regimen that keeps you in shape will make you a more energized and effective shepherd.

Remember, others are watching you. You are their spiritual role model. They will take their cues from you. As crucial as it is for a pastor to model *good financial stewardship* for the benefit of his people, so too he must model *good stewardship of the body.* Leading the way in caring for one's body is a legitimate and underappreciated aspect of pastoral leadership.

One thing more: remember, the cincture is to go across the stomach, not under it.

So, find something. Begin somewhere. And keep at it. Long ago, in a college gymnasium far away I saw a poster that should drive your diet and exercise philosophy, "It is easier to stay in shape than get in shape."

## ON FASTING

Much has been written in many places, not the least of which in the Bible, on fasting. Read up on it.

Did you ever have anyone at the seminary encourage you to seriously consider fasting as part of a regular spiritual discipline? Neither did I; but I am now.

*Seriously consider fasting as part of a regular spiritual discipline.* Fasting serves as a key tool toward significance in ministry.

### FORM OF FASTING

There are many different forms of fasting. You could eliminate one particular kind of food from your diet for a specified time. You could eat only bread and water for a day or a number of days. You could skip a meal or two.

I use a modified sun-up to sun-down approach. Once a week I do not eat anything after whatever snack I might have had in the previous evening until dinner time the next day. It works out to not eating breakfast or lunch or any snacks for a day. This takes place generally on Monday, unless some special food is being planned by someone (birthday of a fellow staff member, lunch with a member, conference), then my fast will happen on Tuesday or Wednesday. On a fast day I limit myself to water and coffee—there is nothing spiritual about caffeine withdrawal!

*How* you fast is secondary to *that* you fast. Fasting in all its forms rests in the realm of adiaphora.

## PURPOSE OF FASTING

Fasting will loosen your grip on the world and tighten your grip on God. You will learn the truth of Jesus' retort to Satan, "Man does not live by bread alone but by every word that proceeds from the mouth of God." (Matthew 4:3) You will come to see "how little" a thing food is compared to the surpassing greatness of God.

Fasting will free you. Food controls our lives more than we realize. Food is to the body what money is to the spirit. Too easily we let these gifts from God become gods in our life. Fasting serves to put food on notice that we will not be servant to it: we serve a living God not a table full of food.

Although it may help you to learn to control your eating the rest of the week, fasting is not dieting. It is spiritual discipline.

Make sure you intentionally connect your fasting with God. On your fast days spend extra time with God in his Word and in prayer. Let the pangs in your stomach serve to teach your heart to yearn for the Lord.

## DEMEANOR OF FASTING

Jesus teaches that fasting should be done in secret. It is between you and God. Do not wear your fasting on your face or make a big deal of it to others.

Actually, the fewer people who know about your fasting the better. If someone invites you to lunch, gently demur and see if there is another day. Don't say, "I'd like to, but this is my weekly fast." If treats are out in the office, don't bemoan the fact saying, "This always happens on my fast day." Just walk by them.

Jesus says, "Put oil on your head and wash your face, so that it will not be obvious to men that you are fasting." (Matthew 6:17) Your fast day should not be readily apparent to anyone else. Let this be a time of intimacy with God, a secret that only you and he share.

### REWARD OF FASTING?

Jesus speaks about a reward when we fast. After he instructed his followers about the oil and the face washing, he continued, "…but only to your Father, who is unseen; and your Father, who sees what is done in secret, will reward you." (Matthew 6:18)

What is the reward that comes with fasting?

Paul wrote a similar thing in his letter to Timothy. "For physical training is of some value (dieting), but godliness (fasting) has value for all things, holding promise for the present life and the life to come." (1 Timothy 4:8)

What is the promise that grows out of the godly practice of fasting? Will it move you toward significance?

There is only one way to find out the answer….

---

## ON MEMORIZATION OF SCRIPTURE

Memorization of Scripture is an ancient practice. Almost as ancient is complaining about it!

Somewhere I read something about the benefits of memorization. The author said, "Bible memorization is a good way to have good things stuck in your head."

Better yet, someone else has suggested that we replace the word "memorization" with the phrase "learn by heart." Yes, that is a good picture: learn the Word of God *by heart*. Now that will head you toward significance.

Let me encourage you to work on the discipline of memorization in two ways.

*First, make sure that Bible memorization is a regular part of your instruction of others.*

Make the catechism students do it no matter how much they complain. Such complaints are eternal. The fact is almost no one *cannot* memorize. Some have to work more than others, but almost everyone can develop this ability—given a little time and effort. *Don't give in to the parents who insist, "My Joey can't memorize."* Patiently, show them otherwise. It will make an eternal difference.

But don't just focus on the catechism kids. Encourage the habit of Bible memorization in the younger children and adults too. Maybe develop a list of key Bible passages that you want everyone in the congregation to know. Don't hesitate emphasizing the same ones over and over. Introduce a passage for the whole congregation to memorize during Advent or Lent or Epiphany Season. Remember, the trick is to help people work at a passage long enough to transfer the information from the short-term memory to the long-term.

*Second, make sure you are working on Bible memorization as well.*

This is a place to lead by example. More and more memorized Bible passages rolling around in your heart and mind will make it more likely that one will bubble up at just the right time in counseling sessions, Bible classes, sermons and witnessing opportunities.

Sometime ago I saw a pastor who started every service with a memorized Bible passage appropriate for the theme of the day. That seemed like a good practice to adopt. So, I did. Every week I begin the service with a memorized portion of Scripture. Sure, some of these passages only end up in my short-term memory. But having done this now for years, more and more have snuck into my long-term memory.

Now that's a fringe benefit from being a pastor! And think how much more powerful starting a service with a memorized portion of Scripture is compared to, "Well, how was your week?" Or "How about the weather?" Or "How about the (insert the name of your favorite team here)?"

What about those who say, "Learning by rote doesn't mean you understand what you have memorized"? Granted. Memorization is not the same as understanding. But the two are not disconnected. In fact, you can't really understand something without having the right words right. You have to get the words down *before* you can get the meaning. And what kind of meaning can there be if you never have the words right?

As you memorize you will find yourself finding new ways of understanding passages as well. You will emphasize different words and see how they fit together. You will not just be getting the words right, but you will also be getting more of the them fitting together in ever richer, significant ways.

I like to think of memorization as loading up the heart and mind with lots of software that can be used at a later time.

One more thing. Don't forget there are other good things to memorize: your church's catechism, hymns, poems, famous quotes, your wife's birthday.

---

## ON DRINKING

I do not mean the ubiquitous water bottle.

I mean alcohol. Beer. Wine. Liquor. This is a touchy topic. But it is one that must be touched.

Make no mistake: alcohol is a gift from God. It is at the heart of our sacramental union with Christ. It is at the center of Paradise's promise. (Isaiah 25:6)

But it also can be and is a problem for the pastoral ministry.

*Watch it.*

Appropriate alcohol consumption rests between Baptists and Lutherans.

*Watch it.*

Too much drinking makes you sloppy. Too much drinking makes you more careless with other sin. Too much drinking makes you a bore. (Drinking ultimately becomes a very self-centered activity.) Too much drinking makes you susceptible to the negative impact of genetic predispositions for alcohol problems.

*Watch it!*

And remember, everyone else is watching you.

*Watch it!!*

Don't let the brevity of this confuse you about its significance.

### Conversation: Disciplines of Person

BIBLE CONVERSATION:

Read 1 Timothy 4:6-9. How does this passage support the importance of the four topics just completed?

FOR PERSONAL REFLECTION:

- Describe your diet and exercise regimen. Where is it strong? Where could it be adjusted? Where does fasting fit in?

- Describe your memorization regimen.

- Describe your alcohol "regimen."

FOR GROUP DISCUSSION:

- Discuss the congregation's culture of eating and drinking. Does it contribute to a godlier congregation?

- What can the congregation do to support the pastor in a more disciplined life?

- What expectations do leaders have about encouraging each other to grow in a more ingrained understanding of the Scripture?

GOING FORWARD:

- Identify one area of concentration for the pastor.

- Identify one area of concentration for the elders or other leadership group.

PRAYER POINTS FOR THE COMING MONTH:

CHAPTER FIVE

# PASTORAL HABITS

Habits can be good or bad. Habits are ingrained patterns of behavior. Good habits can lead toward significance in ministry. Bad habits can lead to disaster, albeit imperceptibly at times. While experts disagree on how long it takes to build a habit, they agree it takes both time and, at least for good ones, attention.

This chapter will explore four "pastoral habits." These differ from tricks of the trade and disciplines of person because they focus more on relationships with other people than tasks (tricks of the trade) or self (disciplines of person).

## ON TALKING ABOUT MEMBERS

Pastors must preserve the good name of parishioners. It's in the Eighth Commandment. A wise pastor early in my ministry gave me one of the greatest lessons on talking about members. Someone was slicing and dicing a member, and this now-sainted pastor said, "I don't know. If I had been through what he is going through, I probably would be the same way." How you talk about members will make a significant difference in the overall culture of your congregation.

*Guard how you talk about dissenters.* Some people are going to disagree with you on things. Some people are going to disagree a lot with you on a lot of things. People are people too. We are easily tempted to vilify people who have divergent opinions. God calls his people sheep. He never calls his people alligators; neither should his pastors, even if the people are acting like it. We are to put the *best construction* on people, not *derogatory names*.

*Guard how you talk about counselees.* Never betray a confidence. Don't use a counselee as a sermon illustration, even anonymously. Someone will put two and two together. Don't let the camaraderie of your staff weaken your resolve not to share interesting tidbits about members you are counseling. Again, even if it is anonymous, don't burden your wife with details of a recent "session." She doesn't need the burden and is probably better at adding two and two than anyone else.

*Guard how you talk about the details of a recent church meeting.* Most church meetings are at least in theory "open meetings," although not many people attend a church meeting that they don't have to attend. But just because they are "open" doesn't give you the right to share every bone-headed thing that someone said about someone else. Church meetings tend to be filled with passion and with tired people. Things get said. Some of the things should have remained unsaid. Don't repeat them. Don't share who was on what side of which issue. Let it rest. Let it go.

*Guard how you talk with other pastors.* Pastors don't appreciate it when members from various congregations get together and enjoy a little "roasted pastor." So, pastors shouldn't do it to the parishioners! Talking about your members in a negative way with another pastor is bound to come back to haunt you. Someone always knows someone else who is related on the mother's side twice removed. Words have a way of being shared and shared and shared. A pastor's wife once told me, "Never say anything that you don't want repeated." Keep that in mind when you are meeting with other pastors.

*Guard how you talk about people in the office. (Part I)* This is another great place to be reminded not to say something you don't want repeated. There is no place in the office for gossip about members. There is a fine line between sharing something with another staff member about a person for ministry purposes and gossiping about that person. When in doubt, keep it to yourself. Make sure that staff prayer time does not degenerate into airing someone else's dirty laundry. The church office is a great place to put into practice what Paul wrote to the Philippians, "Finally, brothers, whatever is true, whatever is noble, whatever is right, whatever is pure, whatever is lovely, whatever is admirable, if anything is excellent or praiseworthy, think about such things." (Philippians 4:8) And talk about them, too.

*Guard how you talk about people in the office. (Part II)* You need to watch how you talk about *people in the office*, meaning the other people on your staff. They tend to be members. You tend to know them better than you know non-staff members. And other members tend to want to get the "low down" on them. Someone at a dinner party or at a golf outing may tempt you to serve up something juicy on a fellow staff member. Resist that temptation. Philippians 4:8 applies here as well.

*One more thing.* There is a great side benefit to guarding how you talk about members. When you are careful about how you talk about others, people will be far less likely to say unkind, untrue or unflattering things about you! After all you are the pastor; people will follow your lead.

## ON LISTENING

Here is one of the most troubling and difficult passages for me. "Be quick to listen and slow to speak." (James 1:19) Are you kidding me? That's a lot to ask from a pastor! Listening is lots harder than it looks.

Surely you know the old line, "There's a reason God gave you two ears but only one mouth." Old lines often get to be old lines because they have a good deal of truth to them.

Learning to listen well will enrich and enhance your effectiveness as a pastor like few other things.

*Listen when laypeople tell you things.* Remember, lay people are people too! They have the Spirit of God in them. They know things. They read things. You will be amazed what you can learn from your parishioners if you take time to really listen. Work at engaging your ears and shifting your mouth into neutral.

*Listen when you are counseling.* Conclusion jumping plagues all the professions. Our past experiences shape our assessment of new situations. All professionals begin to jump to conclusions. Doctors do it. So do lawyers. I saw a statistic in "Blink" by Malcom Gladwell that said doctors tend to jump to a conclusion about a diagnosis after only ninety seconds of listening. Ninety seconds?!? Sickness diagnosed. Course of treatment set. Listening done.

Surely over time professionals will and must generalize about people and their situations. We *should* learn from experience. But ninety seconds? Caution: when you are counseling, listen. And give it more than a minute and a half.

*Listen when you are standing and talking with someone in the narthex.* Quit worrying about what you have to do next. Stop looking around for who you need to talk to next. Focus. You are doing the one thing needful now for that person when you take the time to really listen.

*Listen when you are at a crummy conference.* Sometimes in the midst of what seems to be an aimless, never-ending presentation, you will find a nugget of gold that you will remember forever. Be thankful for that since it is unlikely that you would keep any more than one nugget even from a good conference anyway. So focus. Resist the urge to join the ad hoc meeting out in the lobby. You might be surprised at what gold you will find if you take time to really listen even to a crummy speaker. (Remember, we hope that our congregation does the same on Sunday mornings.)

*Listen when older pastors are talking.* Because there is nothing new under the sun, you can learn a lot from listening to those who have already spent more time under it than you have. Older pastors will share some of the most helpful things you'll ever learn about ministry—if you take the time to really listen. Don't skip local clergy clusters. Do seek counsel from pastors more experienced than you.

*Listen to God.* You hear from God a lot. You hear him in his Word. He speaks through the working of your memory. He speaks through other Christians. He speaks through situations. God speaks to us a lot. The thing is to listen to *him*.

*And of course, listen to your wife.* Listen to what she says *with words*. Listen to what she says *without them*. There is no one in your life who is more interested in your well-being than she. To state the obvious, but to state it: you must be with your wife to really hear her. *Effective listening takes physical presence.* Great listening locations are the breakfast, lunch or dinner table, the weekly night out, the evening strolls, the back patio or the porch in front. Indeed, listen to your wife. You'll be a wiser man, a better husband and father and on a better path toward significance as pastor when you take the time to really listen.

---

## ON WORDS TO WATCH

Words are our ware.

Beware the words. Beware the imprecise use of words.

Here are three words that lead to trouble.

### THE PROBLEM OF PRIDE

Watch *pride*, the word.

Everyone seems to be proud. Victorious sports teams celebrate with *pride*. Parents speak with *pride* about their children's accomplishments. Companies that seek success do so by instilling *pride* in their workers. *Pride* is everywhere, and everyone has it.

While Americans reject what most of history has deemed virtues, we have exalted one historical vice and proclaimed it to be the virtue above all virtues: pride. Gotta have pride!

Watch *pride*, the word. The proverb is not without substance: *pride does come before the fall.* (Proverbs 16:18) At the heart of most ancient tragedies, you will find pride or, as the ancients labeled it, hubris.

Pride focuses on self and personal accomplishment. Pride claims merit or worth by the one who is proud. Pride shows itself in boasting.

Pride dwelt in the heart of the first sin: *we shall be like God.* (Genesis 3:5)

Sure, when people use the word *pride,* they often, but not as often as you might think, do not mean hubris. Maybe we are "happy" that our team won. Maybe we are "thankful" that the kids did well in school. Maybe we are "tickled" that work has gone so well. If that's what we mean, then we should use those words. Be precise in expressing what you mean. The unseemly side of pride always lurks behind the most casual use of the word.

Paul, speaking against pride, wrote, "Let him who boasts boast in the Lord." (1 Corinthians 1:31) As a representative of Jesus, you want all you do to bring attention to him, not to yourself. You want to encourage your congregation to do the same.

Avoiding *pride*, the word, will help you to avoid pride, the sin. Find another word. Do all that you can to eliminate the word from your daily language and your reactions to life's experiences. You will be surprised what a challenge this is. Choose from these words instead: glad, thankful, happy, surprised, tickled, excited.

## THE PROBLEM OF FUN

*Fun* has become the measure of everything. Listen carefully to the culture for a day and hear how often fun is mentioned. Things must be fun if they are to be viewed as having value or worth. Whatever it is, if it isn't fun, it isn't good. Whatever it is, no matter how bad it might be, if it is fun, it is good.

School has to be *fun*. Family life has to be *fun*. Worship has to be *fun*.

If *fun* is indeed the measure of all things, many *good* things are dead in the water.

Don't over hear me. I am not suggesting that school and family life and worship have to be miserable or that it is bad if they happen to be fun. I am suggesting that a thing's value should not be determined by the relative presence or lack of fun.

It is a shame that teachers must first figure out how to make teaching fun before they can focus on student learning. If your confirmation class always has to be fun, you are toast. Marriages built on fun will crumble. Fun drives the disastrous preoccupation that our culture has with games and sports. We live in a land at play.

Being driven by the need for fun is closely connected with narcissism, which is a close cousin to hubris, which is a full-blown version of pride. Hmmmm....

Avoid *fun*. Say you had a *good time*. Share an *enjoyable experience*. When preaching or teaching, do in fact do what you can to *gain and maintain interest,* but don't worry about making it fun. Find a different word and a different goal than *fun*.*

### THE PROBLEM OF TRY

*Try* too? Can the word *try* be a bad word? What in the world can be wrong with the word *try*?!?

*Try* reigns supreme in the realm of weasel words! *Try* is like a get out of jail free card.

Sure, I will *try* to come to your party. (Now you are free to blow it off, since you "tried" to get there.) I promise I will *try* to get the work done by tomorrow. (Now there is no accountability or predictability about that work—or the worker! The promise was only to try.) I will *try* harder next time to be better. (This is neither an apology for failing nor a commitment not to fail in the future.)

As pastors we must be dependable. We must be true to our word. When we give it, we must mean it and fulfill it. If you cannot commit to something without using the word *try*, do not commit to it. Live by the words "Under-promise and over-deliver." Or as that great philosopher Yoda said, "Do or do not; there is no *try*."

Three simple words: *pride, fun, try*. Eliminating them from your everyday vocabulary or using them only sparingly and intentionally will add significance and power to all that you do.

Never ever forget words are our ware. Use them well. Use them carefully.

*For further reading: "Amusing Ourselves to Death," Neil Postman.

---

## ON RECOGNITION

Pastors are notorious for being lone rangers. They are, unfortunately, notorious for being narcissistic. We fall far too easily into the sinfully silly notion that we are the show. We are not. Or that it is about us. It is not.

We must *work* at the recognition that we are in the ministry together with lots of other people. We must *work* at keeping this awareness in our minds and in our habits.

Start there: *recognize* that it is not about you and that you need the involvement of others. *Recognize* that you are not the only one with a brain. *Recognize* that you are not the only one with a good idea. See the other people around you. Listen to the other people around you.

Two things will help you to keep this awareness:

- Look at people when they are talking to you. Do not look for who you will talk to next. Do not look for or what you have to do next. See the people you are talking to when you are talking to them.

- Do not respond to people until they have finished speaking and you have taken a moment to consider what they have said.

It is odd but true: the more people you have around you, the more invisible they will all become. *Work at recognizing the people around you.*

And then give them recognition!

People give pastors lots of recognition. They give us congratulations for a good sermon. They give us honorariums when we marry or bury a loved one. They send us notes of thanks. They give gifts at Christmas, Easter and the like. When a member introduces us to a friend, they give us recognition, "This is my pastor." If you think about it, there is no other vocation that receives the kind of regular recognition that pastors receive. (Maybe this truth is what, humanly speaking, draws somewhat narcissistic people into the pastorate.)

As we have freely received, let us freely give. *Having recognized the impact of others, give recognition to them.*

Find ways regularly to recognize the help, participation and contribution of others.

- Thank you notes from the pastor are a must.
- Phone people up and let them know they are appreciated.
- Have a luncheon for office volunteers.
- Have a "Ministry Celebration Sunday" where you recognize volunteers.
- Send birthday or anniversary cards to leaders.
- Clip newspaper articles that highlight a member's activity and pass them on with a note of congratulations.
- Lift up prayers of thanks.
- Seek to recognize those who do not seek recognition.
- Don't forget to recognize the contributions of your wife. Stop on the way home for flowers once in a while.

One of the first leadership phrases I ever heard, and one of the most significant, is this: *What gets recognized gets repeated.*

### Conversation: Pastoral Habits

BIBLE CONVERSATION:

Read James 3:1-11. How does this passage support the importance of the four topics just completed?

FOR PERSONAL REFLECTION:

- What particular practices do you have in place to maintain confidentiality?

- What do you think are key characteristics of being a good listener? Do you exhibit them regularly?

- Who has been helpful in giving you appropriate affirmation and recognition? What can you learn from what helps encourage you to encourage others?

FOR GROUP DISCUSSION:

- What is your congregation's culture relative to gossip?

- The chapter identified three words to avoid: pride, fun and try. Do you agree? Are there other words whose overuse or misuse works against your congregation's life?

- What plan does your congregation have to regularly give staff, volunteers and other members proper recognition?

GOING FORWARD:

- Identify one area of concentration for the pastor.
- Identify one area of concentration for the elders or other leadership group.

PRAYER POINTS FOR THE COMING MONTH:

## CHAPTER SIX

# HOUSEHOLD HELPERS

"House" and "home" are not quite synonyms. A somewhat obscure and occasionally demeaned poet, Edgar A. Guest, wrote, "Home ain't a place that gold can buy or get up in a minute; Afore it's home there's got t'be a heap o'living in it." A house is a structure; a home is a sanctuary. For pastors to serve well in the Lord's sanctuary, they have to mind well the family.

Family life for a pastor and his family includes the pitfalls of all families' lives with a few others thrown in. This chapter serves to assist pastors in the significant work of making their houses homes. It will also help to keep them from making them idols.

---

## ON FAMILY TIME

To state the obvious: you must make sure that you spend time with your family, corporately and individually. Daily, weekly and seasonally, e.g. vacations, you need to be with the family and they need to be with you. You neglect this to the detriment of all: yourself, your family, your ministry.

Having stated the obvious, let me address this issue from a somewhat contrarian point. Don't let your family become an idol or an excuse for neglecting your congregation. In the last generation or so it has become increasingly fashionable for pastors to "wear their families on their sleeves." We proclaim our date night to everyone. We make missing a meeting for a sports event or a concert a kind of badge of honor. We follow nothing so religiously as the sanctity of our "family day off."

Don't over play "family time." The "family time" pendulum has swung too far in many cases.

Lots of people have jobs that keep them busy and away from their families. I've known many auto workers who regularly work sixty hours a week. Insurance and real estate agents have lots of evening appointments. Retail workers work when "everyone else" is off. And after these people have worked a long week, their pastors still expect them to come to meetings, Bible studies and services at church.

So as a pastor don't get caught up in counting your hours. If you are looking for a forty-hour, nine-to-five gig where you can have every evening at home and every weekend free, this isn't it.

I like what Cicero said, "Duties don't conflict." As a pagan philosopher he may not be all right, but he is not all wrong. Generally speaking, there is enough time in most days and seasons to fulfill your proper duties as a husband, father, pastor, neighbor, citizen. But you had better keep your feet moving.

Here are some tips on how to maximize your time in ways that enable you to properly fulfill your responsibilities at home and get the job done at work:

- *Wherever you are, be fully there.* When you are at work, work.

When you are with the family, be home. I make it my practice to change from my "pastor clothes" to my "family clothes" whenever I come home, even if I have to go back to church in just a couple of hours and change clothes again.

- *Minimize additional activities.* Be careful about classes and sports leagues. Don't enroll in too many. Instead find clever, time efficient ways to keep yourself educationally current and physically fit. While it is good to be involved in the community and beyond, be judicious with the number of community and denominational organizations you join. *Just because you can do an activity, it doesn't mean you should.* Avoid additional hobbies that separate you from your family; instead choose hobbies that bring your family together.

- *Figure out how to milk the clock.* See how to re-utilize time so that you can stretch the day's twenty-four hours. Can you stay up just a little later or get up a little earlier to get something done? What about shortening or skipping your lunch hour? (Many of us pastors would find a double benefit in this!) Set some meetings at non-traditional times; breakfast meetings and late afternoon meetings can free up evenings for everyone. (Your church leaders have families too, and jobs.) Work smart. Work fast. And when you're at work, get at it, get done and get home. Don't make your family or your congregation pay because you aren't diligent in your work habits.

- *Pray.* Although I have yet to find the quote, it has often been said that Luther prayed for two hours a day and, when he got really busy, he prayed for three. Hmmm… Maybe we pastors struggle balancing family time and pastor time because we do not invest enough time in prayer. It sure worked for Luther: he wrote a shelfful of books, led the Reformation, raised a large family and still had time to enjoy a beer with the boys.

- *Turn off the TV and other electronic gadgets.* I envy the people who watch no TV. That is a bar I have not been able to clear. My consolation is that watching TV keeps me connected to the culture. Or is that an excuse? Regardless, watching TV, surfing the net and playing video games can gobble up time like nothing else. And no one, no one is really served. So, every chance you get, turn it/them off.

- *Take your vacation.* There is no godly reason not to. And take it in big clumps. I wish we had taken more vacations two and three weeks at a time. When you go, don't take whatever is the latest communication device with you. Go silent. Go unplugged. Go acoustic. But go!

Yes, balancing well family time and work time will be crucial for your ministry… and family… to head toward significance. Make sure you ride that pendulum carefully.

## ON HOLIDAYS

Holidays are hard. Unless you come from a pastor's family, I am not sure there is any way really to be prepared for how hard the holidays are for a pastor. I know I wasn't.

This is not to whine, but it must be brought out into the open. If you do not deal well with the special challenges of "pastoring" through the holidays, you and yours will be miserable during what are otherwise some great times of the year.

*Holidays call for extra work.* You may have noticed this for the first time on Thanksgiving Eve about 3:00 p.m. your first year as a pastor. You were steeling yourself in final preparation for the evening service, beginning to think ahead to Sunday's Bible class and sermon as well, and it occurred to you that this was the time that your folks began to relax for a long Thanksgiving weekend. Not only did you not get a long Thanksgiving weekend, but you ended up with more to do than in a normal week and with less time to do it.

I am afraid you had better get used to this. Christmas and New Year's Eve are even more this way. Easter, even with all the victory, is no better.

*Holidays carry high expectations.* People expect your best during the holidays. The pews are packed. People look forward to the holidays and expect warmth, wisdom and whimsy in their worship. Bring your A-game. Plus, you see some of the people you see only a couple times a year. If you are going to make an impact, now is the time.

*Holidays hold tired themes.* Admittedly the themes for the holidays are big ones: thankfulness, incarnation, naming of Jesus, his baptism, transfiguration, crucifixion, resurrection, ascension, the outpouring of the Holy Spirit and so on. Yet, because they are the same every year, they can become stale and tired—at least in the preacher's mind. What can you say about Christmas in your twentieth year that you did not say in your second? And what can you say to a faithful follower of Jesus Easter after Easter after Easter. "He is risen! He is risen (yawn) indeed?"

*Holidays are hard on your family.* Just when your family wants to spend time with you in celebration and relaxation, you are preoccupied or pooped. The time that they are least interested in sharing you is the time that you are most in demand by the congregation. Expect emergency calls—holiday stresses come to fruition in families already frayed, and your phone will ring, "Pastor, you have to help me, I don't know where to turn."

Holiday commitments impact your extended family too. They may want to get together for Christmas Day, just like they have for years, and you are unavailable until the twenty-sixth or twenty-seventh. That ten-day get-away holiday vacation you took as a family growing up? Forget about it.

*How to Handle the Holidays?* Keep the following in mind as you navigate through the holidays toward significance:

- *Plan Ahead:* The date of the holiday is no surprise. You know months in advance exactly when it is. Plan ahead and get done what you can before the crush of the holiday itself.

- *Read and Think*: It takes work to keep your preaching and teaching fresh. Make sure you read new things and think from different angles about whatever holiday is in your crosshairs.

- *Create Trade-Offs*: Try to figure out trade-offs that you can make with your family. Very early on we found that Santa could come a day early for a pastor's family. A little later we took the kids to a hotel with games and a pool the weekend after New Year's when I could be *fully* there. Negotiate out what works for your family.

- *Accept the Short End of the Stick*: It is *yours*, not your family's. It is *yours*, not your congregation's. God called *YOU* to be the pastor. If you have to get up early or stay up late, do it. Figure out ways that you can get the work done with as little additional impact on your family as you can. When you feel like whining, don't. You need to be a big boy.

- *Pray with Thanksgiving*: Ask God to guide all of your preaching and teaching. Thank him for the privilege of being his spokesman during such important, albeit busy, times. Thank him for your family, and pray for his wisdom in balancing family and congregational duties.

- *Special Note*: Holidays include celebrations with family and members. Never ever enter the chancel or pulpit when you have been drinking any alcohol.

Through it all keep in mind what Paul writes in Philippians 4:13, "I can do everything though him who gives me strength."

And celebrate! God is good, and it's the holidays!

## ON BEING A HOME-GOING PASTOR

Not everything you learned in seminary is true or helpful. Certainly, the Bible is both. But some of the things the professors said are neither. Your professors were learned, not infallible.

This section deals with a topic I never found to be true, or at least not particularly helpful or complete.

"A home-going pastor makes for a church-going people." You would hear this parroted at the seminary from people who had not been in the parish for a long time or in a long time. I am not sure that there is a shred of evidence that there is a shred of truth about it—at least not in a statistical sense.

For a number of my early years I tried to be that home-going pastor. After dinner I would dutifully head out to make two or three home visits. *I ended up in homes that didn't really need or want me in them and not in the one that did.*

Being a home-going pastor takes lots of time. Lots. And not everyone wants the pastor in the house anyway. Being a home-going pastor is a highly ineffective and often very intrusive approach to ministry.

Certainly, there is a point.

To be an effective pastor you must be connected to people. You will make little progress toward significance in ministry without building strong personal connections with your congregants. While making annual home visitations to everyone in the congregation is probably not a good idea no matter how many faculty members endorsed it, you must have a strategy for connecting with people.

Here are some ways that you can be in touch with people, "be in peoples' homes," without having to go there.

### WRITE NOTES

Notes get you in the house. Except for bills and junk mail, people still like to get mail, real mail.

Drop people notes for all kinds of things:

- Send a note of congratulations for awards, accomplishments or promotions.

- Be liberal with thank you notes, very liberal. Thank people for help in ministry. Thank people for good comments at meetings and Bible classes. *And of course, like your mother taught you, always send thank you notes for gifts of any kind or any value.*

- Drop a note to people for the first Christmas, Easter and anniversary following a loved one's death.

- Let people know that you were praying for them.

## MAKE PHONE CALLS

Phone calls get you connected to people in homes, cars, grocery stores, sporting events. Call people to follow up on a hospitalization or a medical procedure. Call people who you think might be struggling with something; let them know you were thinking about them and give them a chance to share. Call people who you have had difficulty with and give them a chance to air things out. (See note at the end.)

Don't call at dinner time, before 9:00 a.m. or after 9:00 p.m. If you are calling during work, make sure that they can take the call at work. If not, call later.

## VISIT AT THE HOSPITAL

People may not want you in their homes, but they do want you at their side when at the hospital. Make sure that you see them there. Don't stay long. Don't step on air hoses or other tubes.

## BE AVAILABLE BEFORE AND AFTER WORSHIP

Don't hide in the sacristy. One of the best chances you will get all week long to make good contact with people is before and after worship.

Hang out in the narthex. View the narthex as the congregation's shared family room.

## OPEN DOOR POLICY

Be available and willing to see people in your office. If someone makes a special trip by your church to "just see if the pastor is in," that person needs to talk. Set aside what you are doing and talk. Make them feel at home. Appointments are nice but not always possible.

## LATEST TECHNOLOGY

Use it. Emailing and texting are still big enough. Twitter and Facebook too. Who knows what will be next.

Whatever technology you use to connect with people, make sure that you use it in a *personal way* (form letters whether sent through the US mail or email are not personal) and *proactive way* (have it go to the people, don't make them find it on their own).

## AND DO VISIT IN PEOPLE'S HOMES

None of this is an excuse not to visit in people's homes. There are times that you need to be with a person in that person's home. Be there.

The home visit is a good club to have in your bag; it is not the only one, and generally not the most efficient or effective one. But when it's the right club, there is none better.

*NOTE: Keep in mind that when you are conflicted with someone, and there are those times, the more personal you can make the connection, the better. Email and phone calls often exacerbate conflict—the communication is too impersonal. A home visit can be very helpful in working through conflict.*

# ON THE LONG HAUL

*Plan to stick with this for a while.*

Being a pastor is a complicated Calling. The more trips you make around the block the more effective you should be—as long as you don't always go around the same block in the same way. Serving as a pastor is one of those things that is more art than science. Rome wasn't built in a day; neither is a fruitful ministry. (Okay, enough clichés.)

Here's the thing: you won't really hit your stride until you are in your fifties. Even if you get off to a great start with lots of effectiveness, there are some things that *only* come with experience. It is in your fifties that energy, information, maturity and insight all start to come together. That doesn't mean that nothing will happen in your twenties, thirties or forties. It does mean that for all your excitement and energy, the best is down the road.

*Plan to stick with this for a while... even when it isn't going well.*

A big part of sticking with it is *sucking it up* and *sticking it out*. If you are on the front end of your ministry, no doubt you have come to understand, to a degree, the challenge of serving as a pastor. Most fellas spend lots of the early years thinking about what else they might do with their lives. I did not become convinced I should be a pastor until after I turned forty.

When you get to those times that you are so confused, hurt, discouraged or intimidated that you want to quit, don't. There will be lots of difficult days in ministry before you hit your stride at fifty (and plenty thereafter as well), but you cannot hit that stride without going through the first twenty-five years. Keep your head down, and your feet moving.

*Plan to stick with this for a while... even if you remain in the same congregation.*

A special kind of a long ministry is *a long pastorate*, that is, to be in one congregation for a long time. Do not assume that changing congregations every five years or so will lead toward significance. Many of the most fruitful pastors with significant ministries have served the same congregation for over twenty-five years. Imagine how well you would get to know the congregation and the community, and they you, if you were to remain in the same locale for such an extended time. You cannot build decades-long relationships in a half dozen years. If God grants to you, which sadly he hasn't to me, to serve all or most of your ministry in one congregation, you will enjoy a special realm of effectiveness.

*Plan to stick with this for a while… even now planning to finish well.*

I do not advocate a "twenty-something" pastor to think about retirement. Keep in mind that retirement at sixty-two or sixty-five is an American novelty. Before you buy in to that, check out Exodus 7:7.

I do advocate though that even at the front end of a ministry you think about how you might want to serve in your sixties and seventies and beyond. Sure, there might be a re-deployment from full-time work, but there is no good reason not to be greatly fruitful well beyond your fifties… unless you shoot yourself in the foot.

Here's how pastors do that:

- They do not build a dynamic, personal relationship with Jesus.
- They do not build strong relationships with their wives and children.
- They have a moral failure.
- They quit reading, learning and developing.
- They eat, drink or smoke too much.
- They do not exercise.
- They quit thinking.

One of the saddest occurrences in the ministry is a pastor who loses his ministry, either actually or de facto, just when he should be entering an extended season of significance. What you do at the beginning and middle of your ministry will largely determine how you will end. A long, fruitful ministry only occurs when pastors build well in the beginning with an eye to a good ending.

*Plan to stick with it for a while.*

### Conversation: Household Helpers

BIBLE CONVERSATION:

Read Ephesians 5:25-33 and Luke 14:25-33. How do these passages support the importance of the four concepts just completed?

FOR PERSONAL REFLECTION:

- What habits are you building with your family that will help you to have a significant ministry?

- What habits are you building with your ministry that will help you to have a great family life?

- Pastors can in effect turn either their ministry or their family—or both—into an idol. Disagree? Agree?

FOR GROUP DISCUSSION:

- What can you do as leaders to ensure that your pastor develops healthy habits with his family?

- Discuss how you as leaders balance work and family… and church volunteer… time.

- Are there areas of ministry where you think your pastor is spending more time than necessary? Less time than necessary?

GOING FORWARD:

- Identify one area of concentration for the pastor.
- Identify one area of concentration for the elders or other leadership group.

PRAYER POINTS FOR THE COMING MONTH:

CHAPTER SEVEN

# BIG THREE PLUS ONE

*P*astors are subject to the temptations and drives that are common to all people. Just because someone becomes a pastor does not make him immune to human failing. He has received a holy calling; that does not automatically make him wholly holy. In fact, as a good friend of mine likes to say, Satan paints a bulls-eye on his chest. And when a pastor falls, the fall-out is catastrophic. Significant ministry for many has sadly been sidetracked by one of the Big Three.

Pastors must be ever vigilant against temptation, especially in the face of the "big three": money, sex and power. This chapter serves to put pastors on notice about the significant danger of these three areas of temptations… and of one more.

## ON MONEY

**DON'T TOUCH IT.**

As pastor in your congregation, it is a good idea never to touch money—the congregation's cash that is.

Money is one of the three great temptations. Many a pastor has lost his ministry and damaged his congregation because he took money that was not his.

Normally small things start this. You have a petty cash fund that you dip into to stretch things out until payday. You will pay it back. But soon the $20 has become $200, and things get out of control. Or maybe you are collecting cash from the youth for a camping trip. You and your wife could use a new tent, so you purchase one out of the youth money, since they will use it too, but it ends up in your garage. A toy purchased with the congregation's money for a children's sermon finds its way into your own child's toy box. Pretty soon you find more and more ways of using the congregation's money for your own purposes.

Don't touch it. Don't have a petty cash folder for your use; a charge card with stringent reporting systems will accomplish much the same purpose. Do not be the one who collects money for trips. Do not be involved in counting the weekly offering. (In another place I have suggested that you ought to know, at least from time to time, how much people give. But you should never be involved in the actual counting.) If someone says, "Pastor, I forgot to put this money into the offering plate, will you put it in for me?" Don't do it. Find an usher or elder to take care of it.

Let this be an inviolable rule: don't touch the congregation's money. Build this boundary. Let it be clear to you and your leaders. There will be other temptations to misuse (which is a euphemism for stealing) money in addition to the temptation that cash presents. Having this boundary will be a good start to keep you above reproach.

### MAKE SURE TWO TOUCH IT.

Even as you must protect yourself from temptation and sloppy practices, so as pastor you must protect others in the congregation from the same.

The key practice for protecting people from the temptation to take money, cash or checks or other funds that are not theirs is to always have at least two people, not from the same household, responsible for dealing with money. There are three applications of this:

- *Counting the Weekly Offering*: Always have teams of at least two people handling the money. Have a pair of people, the elder and head usher perhaps, secure the offering in a counters' bag after service. Have the entire counting team stay together until the counting is completed.

- *Managing the Money:* You may have one person, a church administrator perhaps, who actually manages the congregation's finances, but he should base his reports on totals that can be substantiated by bank records and counters' reports that a second person, normally the treasurer, regularly reviews. The administrator should not be doing any of the offering counting, and if he manages expenses, his own expenditures should be reviewed by another person.

- *Annual Financial Review*: Have an annual internal financial review by a team of at least two people not involved in the congregation's finances on a regular basis. On a less frequent basis you should have a review, compilation or audit by an outside auditor. (Seek the advice of an accountant on this. There are different levels of review. They vary in both complexity and expense.)

## MAKE SURE TO TOUCH IT OFTEN.

Make sure that you preach and teach often about money. Jesus did.

When you preach and teach about money, let your focus be on breaking people's trust in money and building their trust in God. Jesus said (and he meant it!), "No one can serve two masters. Either he will hate the one and love the other, or he will be devoted to one and despise the other. You cannot serve both God and Money." (Matthew 6:24) As pastor you *must* deal with the subject well and regularly. Money, and the things it can buy, is the chief competitor to Jesus for your people's hearts.

People complain about *"always hearing about money"* in church for two reasons:

- *They have an unhealthy love of money,* and they do not like their idolatry attacked.

- *The pastor has an unhealthy love of money,* and he is too focused on what the money can do for him or for the institutional church.

Don't ever apologize for the first of these. Work, pray and tithe like mad to avoid the second of these.

Your mismanaging of money will destroy your ministry's significance in a flash. Properly dealing with money will move it toward significance.

## ON SEX

As pastor you should be building lots of good and lasting relationships. The longer you are a pastor the more you will find that connection with people drives significance in ministry. Humanly speaking, you make it or break it as a pastor depending on whether or not you relate well with other people.

One of the key aspects regarding relationships is having appropriate boundaries. That's the topic of this section, the second of three big topics.

Sex is a gift from God to be enjoyed by a husband and wife. It is indeed a powerful gift. As with all gifts, Satan seeks to get us to misuse and misappropriate it.

### WATCH IT!

You must not fall into sexual immorality. Except for unbelief itself, nothing is more disastrous to a Christian than to engage in sexual immorality. Paul writes, "Flee sexual immorality. All other sins a man commits are outside his body, but he who sins sexually sins against his own body." (1 Corinthians 6:18)

The writer of Proverbs interestingly juxtaposes wisdom with sexual immorality. Nothing is more stupid than getting involved in sexual relations with someone who is not your spouse. The writer describes the wayward man, "All at once he followed her like an ox going to the slaughter, like a deer stepping into a noose till an arrow pierce his liver, like a bird darting into a snare, little knowing it will cost him his life."

(Proverbs 7:22-23)

Sexual immorality will destroy your marriage, your family, your ministry and your relationship with God.

Boundaries are crucial:

- Never counsel a woman with no one else in a nearby office.

- Do not give rides to a woman by yourself.

- Make sure there is a window into your office. (A counseling friend of mine disagrees with this because it interferes somewhat with privacy. Of course, that is the point of it.)

- Be careful about physical contact. The need for physical contact is a human, even incarnational issue. But watch it. Watch the touching. Watch the hugging. This is not to say never touch or hug people—just be careful. Have clear boundaries. I specialize in warm handshakes.

- Avoid the revelation of intimate details of your life with other women.

These boundaries are to protect you from untoward action *toward* another and to protect you from untoward action *by* another.

### DON'T WATCH IT!

Pornography has no place in your life. It is of no benefit to you, your marriage, your family, your ministry or your relationship with God to see a woman besides your wife without clothes.

We live in a hyper-sexualized culture. Suggestive images abound in "main stream" TV shows, internet ads, critically-acclaimed movies. Avoid them even if it leaves you out of the loop with popular culture. For other reasons as well, less is more when it comes to TV watching, surfing the web and keeping up with movies.

Watch what you watch. Don't let your eyes be the gateway to disaster.

#### WATCH IT WITH YOUR LIFE!

Do all you can to enhance your marriage. Spend time with your spouse. Avoid hobbies that make an already busy pastor an absent husband. Eat dinner together without the TV. Go on a date every week—without kids. Share your intimate heart concerns, joys and fears with each other. And as my pastor from long ago said, "If you are too busy for sex, you are too busy."

You may not be married yet. As a single man, how you comport yourself now and the kind of purity habits you practice now will bless your marriage when and if God grants you a spouse. You do not want to begin a marriage filled with regret and shame from past relationships.

As a married man you must keep faith with your wife to be faithful only to her. You gave your word. Do not break it.

I could go on and give more details and more specifics, but this topic could also have been addressed with just two words: *watch it*. That will keep you on the path toward significance.

---

### ON POWER

It is not *hard* to guess that when it comes to temptation and personal failure the big three issues are money, sex and power. Here's what you might not guess: *the biggest of these temptations is power*.

Do not underestimate the power that you have as a pastor. The power you have is independent of the size of your congregation: it comes with your office.

People really listen to you. People really do what you tell them. People really entrust their lives and souls to you.

You are invited into intimate places. You're there for weddings, baptisms, confirmations, graduations and funerals. People share with you their greatest fears and failures. You see bared souls. You know your people in a way that no one else does.

This is powerful stuff. At times you will find this more intoxicating than the most potent liquor. Kids are not the only ones who will think that in your robe you look like Someone Else.

Watch it.

Use this power wisely.

## TO WHAT END?

Keep in mind that the power that you have must be directed toward drawing people closer to Jesus, not aggrandizing yourself. It is not about you.

It is good to remember again John the Baptist's words, "He must increase, and I must decrease." (John 3:30) Jesus cautioned us not to exert our authority over people like the Gentiles did; rather, we are to use our authority to serve one another.

Remember, the position you hold as pastor is for the *Kingdom of God* and not for the *Kingdom of Steve* or *the Kingdom of Ted*. Whenever you find yourself using your position as pastor for personal advancement, back off.

## CHECKS AND BALANCES

For all the foibles of the government of the United States, the thing that makes it work is a very intentional system of checks and balances.

Make sure that you have people who keep you in check and help you to stay balanced.

- *Church Board*: Congregations have different governance systems, but they all have some system. *Insist* that the appropriate body of your governance system (Board of Elders, Board of Directors, etc.) works you through an annual personal goal-setting and evaluation process. *Insist* that they hold you accountable. The pastor who does not do this is an accident waiting to happen.

- *Accountability Group*: Establish a group of people with whom you can have regular conversation about your work. Pick people who will ask tough questions. These can be colleagues. They can be congregants.

- *Local Pastors' Conference*: Don't miss it. You need this group. They need you. If one doesn't exist, create it.

- *Mentor*: Find someone, not necessarily a pastor, who has a decade or two on you. Find someone who will challenge you and in whom you can confide.

- *Wife and Mother*: Listen to the ladies. If you are being a dope or doing something foolish, they will tell you. Listen.

CHECK THE EGO

Make sure that you have ways to keep your ego in check. Practice the following:

- *Listen to Lay People*: You're not the only person who knows things. What your lay people know and what they can do should keep your ego in check—if you listen. However, should they tell you that you are the most wonderful pastor with the best sermons, listen with lots of skepticism.

- *Assume You're Not the First*: If you have a great idea or a great achievement, assume someone else has thought of it before you and done it better. This is not to belittle yourself, but it will keep you from getting too big for your britches. The writer of Ecclesiastes says this very thing, "There is nothing new under the sun." (Ecclesiastes 1:9)

- *Give Glory to God*: Remember, all the really best stuff that you do is from God. Keep in mind that he works in, through and in spite of you.

- *Balaam's Ass*: Whenever you think that your ego is getting out of control, check out Numbers 22.

Both God and his people have entrusted great power to you. Exercise it only as steward and servant. Direct it toward significance; direct it toward Jesus!

## ON TRUTH-TELLING

"I tell you the truth," is a happy translation for the word "amen." "Truly, truly," is pretty good too.

Doesn't it always sound nice to hear Jesus start a statement by, "I tell you the truth..."? He rightly identified himself as the Way, the *Truth* and the Life.

As you know, truth has taken a beating. People are not even sure there is such a thing as truth. They think that truth is simply a cultural construct that is determined by people's point of view. Our culture is driven by a statement that is impossibly contradictory, "There is no such thing as truth."

Our entire faith is dependent both on the existence of truth and that God is the embodiment of it. Every truth grows out of the nature of God.

Satan lies. He is the father of lies. Scripture identifies "Liar-ish" as his native tongue. (John 8:44)

As a servant of the Truth, you must strive to tell the truth. Always.

Of course, this is hard to do. And the harder you try, the bigger bugaboo you will find truth-telling to be. But as a forgiven, restored servant, strive you must.

You must win a reputation for truth-telling beyond your preaching… for the sake of your preaching. People who fib about one thing will fib about another thing. People must be able to trust what you say, always.

Beware the encroachment of falsehood in the following areas:

## WATCH CHURCH STATISTICS AND REPORTS

Falsehood creeps in when pastors talk with other pastors and with congregational leaders about how things are going. We are tempted to inflate the figures just a bit. If we have an average attendance of 330, we will be tempted to say it is just shy of 400. If we have 12 in a new member class, we will be tempted to say it is 15 or so. If offerings are up 2.3%, we will be tempted to say it is about 5%. Force yourself to *avoid exaggeration* and *statistic inflation*. When rounding, get in the habit of rounding down. Brutal and thorough honesty in this area, which is so tough to pull off, will keep truth-telling at the center of your radar. I have often said the quickest way to get a pastor to lie is to ask him for the average worship attendance number of his congregation.

## GIVE CREDIT WHERE CREDIT IS DUE

If you get an idea for a sermon illustration or for a new program or for a powerful quote, make sure that you credit the source. Or at least do not try to pass it off as your own work. Giving false impressions of what you have done is lying. If the story you are telling is not something you experienced first-hand or is not something that you thought of, make sure that you do not make it sound like it was.

## DON'T MAKE EXCUSES

When you are wrong about something or could not complete something, do not make excuses for it. Admit it. Correct it. But don't make excuses. Excuse-making tends to bend the truth and reconstruct the past. That's lying.

## DON'T LIE TO SPARE PEOPLE'S FEELINGS

Lies often pop up because someone doesn't want to hurt another's feelings. Instead of telling the truth, we deceive the person with the supposed goal of being nice to that person?!? Remember, Scripture enjoins us to speak *the truth in love*. (Ephesians 4:15) There is no notion of speaking *a lie in love*! Lying to a person with the supposed goal of "sparing feelings" is like throwing a drowning person a life vest with an anchor attached to it.

## SILENCE IS GOLDEN

One of the best ways to stay on track with the truth is to keep quiet. Instead of telling someone you like her hat when you don't, keep your mouth shut. Instead of making an excuse for why you cannot join a member's social event when the truth is you just need some down time, simply thank them for the invitation and then kindly decline it—no explanation is required. Instead of making something up about a situation with one member when asked by another member, demur by saying that you are not at liberty to comment about it—because you are not.

### REMEMBER THE HOME FRONT

Be vigilant as a truth-teller at home. This includes doing what you say you will do and being where you say you will be. Be forthright with your wife about all things except those things that are confidential, and then be silent. Never deceive your children in order to get them to behave or eat or sleep. Never.

A good reputation is a great treasure. Reputations are earned, not freely acquired. Make sure that you earn a reputation for being a truth-teller. Jesus had that reputation. As his under-shepherd, you must too.

This is a significant work. You will notice that the harder you work at this, the more you will see you need to work at this.

## Conversation: Big Three Plus One

**BIBLE CONVERSATION:**

Read 1 Corinthians 10:1-13 and Matthew 20:20-28. How do these passages support the importance of the four issues just completed?

**FOR PERSONAL REFLECTION:**

- What intentional safeguards do you have in place to protect yourself from temptations related to money and sex?

- What support systems do you have in place to keep power and ego in check?

- How are you earning a reputation for being a truth-teller at work and home?

FOR GROUP DISCUSSION:

- What safeguards does your congregation have in place to protect itself against financial and sexual failings by the pastor, lay-leaders or other members?

- Discuss this statement. "Power is an alien concept to the Church." Agree? Disagree?

- How does your congregation support a culture of truth?

GOING FORWARD:

- Identify one area of concentration for the pastor.

- Identify one area of concentration for the elders or other leadership group.

PRAYER POINTS FOR THE COMING MONTH:

CHAPTER EIGHT

# PROFESSIONAL DUTIES

Historically, three professions existed: law, medicine, theology. They were the literate class. And they had at least one other thing in common, and it wasn't a high salary. Lawyers, doctors and pastors all held "privilege." You could tell them something in confidence, and they would have to keep it in confidence. Today almost anyone who is paid for something is called a professional—the term now means "I get paid for it." "Historical" professions still hold a unique spot in our society and maintain "privilege," and at least one other characteristic: about fifteen hours a week more than most other jobs.

In your capacity as pastor you are a professional. You hold "privilege." You hold a standing in society similar to lawyers and doctors—even if your salary doesn't stand close to theirs. And you will work longer than most other people you know. In your work as pastor there are certain duties, duties of the profession, that will fall to you and that must be done with excellence if you seek significance in ministry.

## ON LEADERSHIP

Your seminary training did not train you to be a leader. It couldn't. Seminary training rightfully focuses on training students to be and think like theologians. While you may have spent some time on leadership development, that is not the point of being at the seminary.

You're not at the seminary anymore. Get yourself leadership training—lots of it.

### PASTOR, NOT CHAPLAIN

Do not confuse your Call as pastor with the functions of a chaplain.

There are certain chaplain functions that must be done: visit the sick, comfort the bereaved, counsel the distraught. Make sure that weddings, baptisms, confirmations, communions and funerals are all conducted decently and in order. Hold hands that need to be held. Rebuke when necessary.

These tasks do not all need to be done by you. Involve elders, fellow staff and other volunteers wherever you can. Share ministry.

These tasks, however, cannot be all you do! You cannot let yourself get so consumed by chaplain functions that you fail to fulfill the crucial role of pastor as leader. Do a word study sometime on the term "shepherd" as used in Scripture. You will find that it tracks closer with the idea of "king" than it does "chaplain."

It is an old leadership issue: there is a difference between "urgent" and "important." When it comes to being a pastor, chaplain functions tend toward urgent; leadership functions tend toward important.

## SINE QUA NON

If you cannot lead, you cannot be a pastor. Pastors have flocks. Flocks are to be led closer to Jesus, in paths of righteousness and on the road to Glory.

Pastors must be theological leaders. They must be servant-hearted leaders. They must be non-dictatorial leaders. (Technically, dictators are not leaders, they are pushers.) But pastors must be leaders!

Again, if you cannot lead, you cannot be a pastor. Without leadership skills you will become an impediment and an irritant. I have seen more congregational conflict grow out of poor leadership skills than faulty theology.

## LIFE-LONG LEADERSHIP TRAINING

Plan to spend the rest of your life learning to be a better leader.

- *Read books on leadership.* Always have a book going on leadership. Always. Read new stuff. Read old stuff. Read biographies. Read about non-profit leadership. Read about for-profit leadership. If leadership skills help companies to make money, shouldn't we learn from those same skills, humanly speaking, to make disciples? (Of course we filter everything according to the Word of God.)

- *Read books on organizations.* Organizational theory is the other half of leadership theory. Organizations are what leaders lead. Never, ever apologize for thinking about your congregation as a corporation. (See 1 Corinthians 12:27)

- *Attend leadership conferences and training events.* Make sure that these are at the top of your continuing education agenda, especially if you are at the beginning of your ministry.

- *Seek feedback from your congregation and its other leaders.* Make sure that you have open dialogue with your congregation about how you are or are not functioning as a leader. Since they are the led, they will know best how you are doing as leader. Never fear feedback. Lay people have tons to teach the pastor. Listening is a big part of leadership.

KEY PINCH POINTS

There are two key areas that pinch pastors. If they are not addressed, they will pinch you right out of the ministry.

One area is moral failure. That has been addressed elsewhere.

The other area is leadership. If you desire a joyful pastorate of significance, study leadership.

## ON PREACHING

Books galore have been written on preaching. Some of them should be read.

There is only one thing you need to know about preaching: *it should be a message from Jesus about Jesus.*

Pretty simple.

Simple, not easy.

Preaching and, even more so, the preparation for preaching is the hardest thing a pastor does all week. You should be prepared weekly to do battle with Satan as you plunge into the Word of God for the good of the people of God. Suit up with the panoply of God.

*It should be a message.* Not a lecture. Not a paper. Not an oratorical wonder. People need to have a word from their God to help their life and to strengthen their faith, hope and love.

*It should be FROM Jesus.* Jesus is the Word. Preach the Word. Preach Jesus from the Word. The best illustrations for sermons will be found in the Bible itself—there are plenty of characters for years of sermons! Use other passages to support your point. Reading through the Bible annually and regularly memorizing Bible passages will buttress your preaching like nothing else.

*It should be ABOUT Jesus.* Make sure your message is really proclaiming the Savior. Remember what Jesus said? "You search the Scriptures because you think that in them you have life. And it is they that testify about me." (John 5:39) So too our sermons should always testify to Jesus: his love, forgiveness, peace and power.

*That means your sermons should not be about you.* Humanly speaking, for preachers to be preachers we must have a little ham bone in us. At a conference somewhere the speaker said, "All preachers are a little narcissistic. They *must be* to get up in front of people on a Sunday morning." So, our nature needs to be on notice. We need to be on guard against *our* getting in the way of *Jesus*: our experiences, our insights, our learnedness and our wit. Sure, we should be "real" and "authentic." Personal experiences, insights, knowledge and witticisms have their place. Preachers must both gain and retain people's attention. But in this area of ministry more than any other we need the spirit of John the Baptist. Remember? "He must increase; and I must decrease." (John 3:30)

*And please, please, leave your family out of it!* The people don't need to hear about how wonderful or quirky or interesting or accomplished your family is. They have family of their own. And your own family doesn't need to have to worry about what slip-up at the dinner table or trouble at school might become the next sermon illustration.

*One more thing: don't lie or deceive.* Remember when we are preaching we are proclaiming the Author of Truth. There should be no falsehoods in our preaching. So, if you are recounting an event that did not happen to you, don't make it sound like it did. If you are saying something witty or insightful that you got from someone else, acknowledge that it's not yours. If you have borrowed someone's story or have made one up, make sure people know it.

*The path toward significant preaching is to share messages from Jesus about Jesus.*

Pretty simple.

Simple, not easy.

---

## ON MEETINGS

I always thought we should change the words from the old hymn Onward Christian Soldiers from "Like a mighty army *moves* the Church of God" to "Like a mighty army *meets* the Church of God."

Why is it that church meetings seem to take forever and go nowhere?

You better get good at meetings. You will have a lot of them: Elders, Church Council, Sunday School teachers, staff, local clergy, worship team, and so on and so on and so on.

### LENGTH

I have heard it said that *nothing good* happens in a meeting after an hour and a half, and *not much good* happens after forty-five minutes. Keep an eye on how long your meetings last. Unlike rock concerts, shorter is better.

Agree before the meeting starts when it will end. The ending time is as important as the beginning time. Hold to the determined ending time. Budget the use of time in accord with the length of the meeting. A clock in the meeting room helps keep things on schedule.

Be especially sensitive to the length of evening meetings. Remember, the folks sitting at the table have already put in a long day and have things to do at home.

AGENDA AND PURPOSE

Don't have a meeting without these. Never. These serve as a contract with and between you and the participants.

And stick to them. If something comes up at the meeting that begins to lead the group toward non-agenda issues, gently, but firmly, lead the group back on track. If there is an issue that must be dealt with, find another time to consider it. If in fact you must deal with the unexpected item "right now," take something else off the agenda by mutual consent.

Make sure that participants know *in advance* of the meeting what the agenda and purpose are. Equip them *in advance* with information that will be helpful in completing the agenda and following the purpose.

DEVOTIONS

While meetings ought to begin and end with the participants seeking God's direction and blessing through prayer, let me encourage you *NOT* to include a Bible study devotion at every meeting.

Devotions that are given at the beginning of meetings tend to be more perfunctory than edifying. Generally, they are hastily prepared. You will find that such devotions encourage participants to straggle into the meeting.

As long as your meeting has a legitimate agenda and purpose, it is a legitimate gathering of the people of God to do the work of the Church even without a Bible study. Although you can't get too much of a good thing, a Bible study is not "necessary" in such situations, especially if neither the agenda nor the purpose of the meeting is Bible study.

Your leaders should already be in the Word. They should be Bible readers. A meeting is a meeting, not a study. This is the time to put the Word into action. It should be the Word at work.

## DECISIONS

When making decisions at a meeting, keep in mind the following:

- Make sure that those affected by the decisions have been in some way included in the consideration. Don't let the Elders make decisions for the Sunday School without the Sunday School volunteers somehow involved.

- The more decisions that can be made by consensus rather than by an actual vote, the better. Votes lead to winners and losers. The fewer of those in the congregation, the better.

- Once a decision has been made, make sure that all stick with it and support it.

## SOCIALIZING

Arrive at meetings a little early and plan to linger a bit afterwards. Socializing and conversation preceding and following a meeting build camaraderie in a group. During the meeting itself, while there should be light-hearted give and take, keep the off-topic conversation to a minimum.

## CHAIR

Not everyone has the knack to chair meetings. When you find people in your congregation who can chair meetings effectively, treasure them. Develop some kind of training or information sheet for all new chairs of boards and committees. Time invested in training chairs of boards and committees pays tremendous dividends for more significant meetings.

## ROBERT'S RULES OF ORDER

Church meetings, because participants feel so passionately about their congregation and because the Enemy does too (from a different point of view), often careen toward the chaotic. They need order.

You may be aware that U.S. Army Major Henry Martyn Robert devised his "Rules of Order" in response to difficulty he met in running a church meeting. Others have experienced the same situation at church meetings. (Note: This is an understatement of extreme proportion.)

Most congregations use "Robert's Rules of Order" to some degree. Often their use is stipulated in organizing documents like constitutions and bylaws. The greatest benefit of The Rules is that, properly applied, The Rules keep one item on the table at a time so that conversation can be focused. You must have a working knowledge of The Rules so that you can use or, when necessary, ignore them.

When using "Robert's Rules of Order", keep in mind the following:

- They are a tool; do not let them become a master. They are to keep a meeting under control; they should not take control of the meeting.

- And don't let them become a club either. Too often a participant at a meeting will invoke "Robert's Rules of Order" in a way that circumvents a healthy give and take and at the same time clubs a dissenter to silence.

- When people begin to invoke "Robert's Rules of Order", the disorder is already at the door. Be careful.

NUMBER TWO

Preaching/teaching is the number one demand on a pastor's time. Meetings are number two. Mastering the art of conducting good and efficient meetings will lead your *congregation toward significance*.

---

## ON PUBLIC PRAYER

One of my anxieties as a beginning pastor was praying publicly. I remember as a freshly minted minister being asked to say the prayer at the potluck after the installation service at my first congregation.

The pressure was on. My wife was present, Mom and Dad too. Area clergy, veterans of many a potluck prayer, stood waiting to hear what kind of fella the seminary was producing these days—would he get all the words right? And the eager faces of the members, heads reverently bowed, betrayed a hopeful prayer of their own that they were getting a good one.

A lot was riding on that first prayer. Lots were listening. Great pressure to get it right for all the assembled!

Then it occurred to me: *I wasn't talking to them.* There was a point of clarity in my mind that first day of ministry that has seldom been equaled since: public prayer, public as it is, is not a performance. Oz Guinness in his book "The Call" reminds us that our audience is One.

When you pray publicly, remember that you are praying *for* the people not *to* them. The thing that matters is bringing issues before God. It is great that the people are joining their hearts with your words, but the connecting with God is what really matters. This is what leads toward significance in public prayer.

*Do not use public prayer to teach your people.* Do not hope that they "get the message" from what you are praying. Sometimes pastors are tempted to "re-preach" the sermon during the Prayer of the Church. Don't give into that temptation. It is fair to pray about what you preached; just keep in mind that you are addressing God *for* the people not making one last ditch effort to get your point across *to* the people.

*Do use public prayer to teach your people.* Kids learn to talk by listening to parents and siblings talk to one another. Parishioners can learn to pray by listening to their pastor talk to God on their behalf. The teaching that you do in the act of public prayer is by example, not as a sermon recap. Your people will learn to pray for the president if you do. Your people will learn to pray for the work of the Church beyond your congregation if you do. Your people will learn to pray for people in need if you do. This is where lex orandi, lex credendi applies.

When you pray publicly, you have two options. You can pray a pre-written prayer, one written by you or someone else, or you can make up a prayer on the spot. Praying "on the spot" is often misidentified as an "ex corde" prayer, one from the heart. That is erroneous. A prayer made up on the spot is not ex corde. It is extemporaneous, one for that time.

Here's the point: *every prayer you pray on behalf of the people should be ex corde*, whether it is an ancient prayer handed down through the centuries for the church or whether it is one you are making up as you go. If you are not praying from the heart, keep the prayer to yourself. Technically, that's exactly what you are doing.

One more thing: this is a good time to remember that your people are body and spirit. Watch that the length of your public prayers takes into account how long your people can kneel or stand during a service—and how long they can withstand the wafting aroma of the church potluck!

### Conversation: Professional Duties

**BIBLE CONVERSATION:**

Read Deuteronomy 17:14-20. How does this passage support the importance of the four sections just completed?

**FOR PERSONAL REFLECTION:**

- How did your seminary education prepare you for leadership and facilitation of meetings? What are you doing to grow in those areas?

- What boundaries do you have in place to make sure that your sermons have the right balance of focus on Jesus and authenticity of the pastor?

- How do you make sure that your prayers, whether pre-written or extemporaneous, are *ex corde*?

**FOR GROUP DISCUSSION:**

- Discuss the various roles your pastor fulfills including leader. What do you expect of him as leader? What don't you expect of him?

- *Carefully and kindly*, discuss with the pastor how his sermons are helpful and how they could be even more so.

- What practices does your congregation have in place to ensure that meetings are both effective and safe from becoming contentious?

GOING FORWARD:

- Identify one area of concentration for the pastor.

- Identify one area of concentration for the elders or other leadership group.

PRAYER POINTS FOR THE COMING MONTH:

CHAPTER NINE

# A LIFE'S ENDEAVOR

There are three things that necessitate you focus on being a life-long learner. First, there was a lot more to learn than the seminary could have taught you during your time there. Mostly, seminary taught you how to continue to learn throughout your pastorate. Second, you will be faced with things neither you nor the seminary could have predicted. The changing climate of ministry necessitates continued education. Third, you need to stay fresh. If you are doing and saying in year twenty of your ministry only what you did in year two, you will become worse than a heretic, you will have become a bore.

Life-long learning will involve reading. Words, not just The Word, are powerful. Life-long learning will involve looking at old things (not everything old is bad) and new things (not everything new is good). Life-long learning will involve effort and discipline. And life-long learning will lead toward significance.

## ON READING

Read lots. Reading is to the brain what eating is to the body.

One of the best ways to *read lots* is to *read a little* every day. Over the course of a forty-five year ministry if you read a little bit every day, it will add up to lots!

*Read the Bible.* Aggressively. Plan to make it through the entire Bible at least once a year. Of all the reading we do, reading Scripture is of first importance. Luther insisted on teaching boys and girls, men and women, to read for this particular purpose.

*Read the "newspaper" and a weekly news magazine.* You need to know what is going on in your community and in the world. You need to "read the culture" in which you minister. Reading newspapers and news magazines will help accomplish this. Many small communities provide a weekly paper. Read it. Big cities often have neighborhood papers. Read them. (As you know, more of these are online and fewer of them are on the front doorstep.)

*Read old stuff.* In his book, "A Contrarian's Guide to Leadership," Stephen Sample encourages people to read only books at least fifty years old. He reasoned that we should let history sift out books that are not worth reading since time for reading is limited. This is good advice. I wish I had followed it more.

*Read new stuff.* This is important not because of *what's new*. We know there is nothing new under the sun. Read new stuff so that you are aware of *what's now*. This will help you converse with your contemporaries.

*Read hard stuff.* Don't worry if you read books that you can barely understand. Such challenges will keep you sharp.

*Read varied stuff.* Check out a book on the human genome. Enjoy one about the Civil War. What about something on economic theory or the geology of the Australian outback? One of my favorite books was one on manners referenced elsewhere in this book, "Miss Manners Rescues Western Civilization." It is especially important to read books that take positions antithetical to what you think or that are in a field totally unknown to you.

*Read novels.* Classic ones. Not so classic ones. Novels will expose you to story-telling. Novels will demonstrate how words impact emotions. Both of these are crucial skills to communication generally and preaching specifically.

*Read leadership books.* Tons of the pastoral calling is leadership. Seminary education must focus on training you as a theologian. Your post-seminary reading regimen must include a focus on training yourself as a leader.

*Read more than one book at a time.* When you have multiple books on your desk and night stand, you are more likely to experience a serendipitous insight.

*Read the funnies.* This is something I have started to do more of. A good laugh is a good thing.

*Read theological works.* Some. Not lots. If you practice all of the above, including aggressive Bible reading, you will have already done lots of theological reading!

*Read.* At the very least, time spent reading will not be time spent watching TV or playing video games.

## ON BOOK CLUBS

You ought to get involved in a book club or two along the way.

A book club will help you read books properly. Mortimer Adler in his book, "How to Read a Book," teaches that there is more to reading a book than reading it—much more. Reading, really reading a book, is a very intentional, multi-step process. It is the kind of process that book clubs generally follow.

Your participation in a book club will discipline you to *READ* books:

- Search out the general direction of the book, author, background, historical situation.

- Read the book. Mark it up liberally—if you own the copy.

- Skim back through it for points worthy of discussion, clarification or criticism.

- Discuss it with others. *This is the book club event.*

- Reflect on its salient points one more time.

There are different kinds of book groups.

*Eclectic Group*: Choose members from various walks of life and faith positions. For a number of years, I have been the weakest member in a group that includes a symphony conductor, a book publisher, a corporate attorney, a hospital president and a lead research scientist. (An architect had to leave the group for a job change.) We do not all hold the same opinions about things. Together we have read through a shelfful of books—most of which I never would have chosen on my own. Reading books with people who think and believe differently than you do will challenge and enrich.

*Collegial Group*: Choose members from your general area of occupation. For even more years than with the above group, I have been meeting with a group of brother pastors with whom I attended college. Annually we select a book germane to our calling, read it in advance and then discuss it over a period of three days. (There might be a little golf, grilling and goofing around in there too.)

*Study Group*: One of the Bible studies at church has developed really into a book group. We read a chapter a week in a book that intersects with the Christian faith and get together to discuss it. We always bring appropriate Bible passages to bear. Discussion seems to flow freer than if we only read chapters of the Bible. A neutral book frees participants to express divergent opinion promoting good discussion without people feeling like heretics.

*Ad Hoc*: This kind of "group" is created by simply passing a good book on to someone else and saying, "You might like this. Let me know what you think." Be careful with this kind of group. That knife can cut both ways. Your friend might return that favor and you will end up with more books to read on your own desk!

*Cliff Note Group*: I have never been in this kind of a group, but I have often thought it would be a good group to start. Each participant would read a different book and write a one page "executive summary." The group would then gather and discuss the various summaries. This way you would be exposed to more books without having to read them. Ecclesiastes 12:12 reminds us, "Of making many books there is no end, and much study wearies the body." A Cliff Note group would help to lighten the burden and still broaden the horizon.

Indeed, pastors must be life-long learners. Reading groups of various sorts will continue to enrich your learning at a fraction of the cost and time of additional degrees or frequent conferences. They are a great help on your path toward significance.

## ON NEW AND OLD THINGS

Decisions. Decisions. Decisions.

Pastors have lots of decisions to make every day. What to do? What not to do? How to do what to do? Why *not* to do what you are *not* doing?

And so on.

As you approach decision making, determining the proper balance of new and old things will serve you well as a decision-making filter.

### NEW THINGS

Start new things in your ministry. Start a new congregation. Start a school or daycare center. Start a new program. Start a new outreach. Start a new ministry.

Starting new things does three things.

*First, it forces you to rethink old things.* How much of the old things do you need to carry over to the new thing? And if you don't need to carry all of the old things into the new thing, should you keep doing all of the old things in the old thing?

*Second, it frees you up from worrying about making mistakes.* Lots of ministry is stifled by the fear of failure. We worry about getting things wrong, making mistakes. That's the beauty of starting a new thing. You can't make a mistake doing a new thing. You can't do a new thing wrong because it hasn't been done before; there is no set way it must be done. Starting new things sets you free from the paralyzing fear of making a mistake. (This isn't completely accurate, but you see the point? Do you sense the freedom?)

*Third, it gets new things started!* Every congregation was started by someone. Someone started every school or ministry or outreach or program. You have benefitted enormously from what other people got started. One of the ways you move your ministry toward significance is by starting something new now for the benefit of someone else later. It's like your grandma said, "Put something back into the pot."

Here's what it takes to get something started:

- an idea
- some gumption
- you

Some prayer sure helps too.

## OLD THINGS

In your ministry you are building on the history of those who have gone before you in your congregation and those who have gone before you through the centuries. A lot of smart, spiritual, capable people worked to get the Church and your congregation where it is today. Don't take the contribution of the past lightly. Tradition does count. G. K. Chesterton calls tradition the "democracy of the dead." Do not confuse old with bad. We do that often enough in America.

Having said that, in ministry some old things should be *continued,* and some old things should be *discontinued.* Put your thinking cap on to sort out which is which.

*Do not change things just to change them.* Zealous pastors run the risk of letting their excitement run roughshod over the past. Assume that there are reasons for why things are the way they are. You may have to investigate to find the reasons so that you understand the status quo. If the reasons are no longer valid, then *perhaps* make changes. But even then, if the change is not *crucial* to move ministry ahead, you might leave things the way they are. Change calls for lots of energy. Chits have to be expended. You only have so much energy and so many chits.

Be very deliberate when it comes to changing things. Beware the law of unintended consequences.

*Do change the old things that need to be changed.* There is a huge difference between being *shaped* by the past and being *paralyzed* by it. Be careful. Make sure those who are affected by the change are involved in the process. But do make the changes. Your congregation depends on you and desires you to shepherd them into fresh and new pastures.

You can find many books on the successful implementation of change. Read some. John Kotter, Jim Collins and Peter Drucker are good places to start.

And so…

Which new things to start and how? Which old things to keep and where? Ah, that's part of the art of being a pastor.

---

## ON EXCELLING

What's the point of not doing your best? What's the point of not trying to get better?

Scripture has some choice words about being a sluggard. Check out Proverbs 6:9-11.

There are two schools of thought. One says to *work hard on your weaknesses* to minimize them. The other says to *work hard on your strengths* to maximize them.

Why not both?

Sure, you will only ever get so strong in an area of inherent weakness. There are some areas of ministry in which you will always struggle. But to whatever degree you can minimize that weakness, your ministry will be the more significant for it.

Other areas of ministry will come easily for you. You seem to be naturally good at them. Do not rest on that natural ability; rather, through continued effort make those areas points of excellence.

Like so many other issues, the key is balance. Regularly spend time sorting out areas of weakness and strength. Figure out a strategic allotment of time and resources to minimize the one and maximize the other for excellence in ministry.

Keep in mind that excellence is developed incrementally. Doing just a little better on a number of things over a long period of time will lead you to it. Take to heart a book title I have mentioned in an earlier chapter, "It Takes So Little to Be Above Average." Isn't that right? Do just a little more. Gut it out just a little longer. Put on just a little more spit and polish. Practice it one more time.

In your zeal to be better, watch the competition. The real idea here is not about being better than another. It is, corny as it sounds, to be the best *you* can be. I heard this somewhere: "Don't worry about being the best in the world; be the best for the world."

Watch also for pride. It is a deadly, destructive sin. Most tragic figures in literature were undone by an area of excellence. Many a leading churchman and congregation have been undone by pride.

*Hone your gift mix toward excellence.* It is God's gift to you, a sacred trust, an edification tool for the Church. This will speed you toward significance.

## Conversation: A Life's Endeavor

**BIBLE CONVERSATION:**

Read Proverbs 6:9-11. How does this passage support the importance of the four topics just completed?

**FOR PERSONAL REFLECTION:**

- Describe your plan for continuing education. What is on your reading list? Who do you have as companions for life-long learning?

- Do you have a bias toward the new and novel or the tried and true? How do you balance engaging in both new and old things?

- Assess your strength and weaknesses. Which could benefit from more attention?

**FOR GROUP DISCUSSION:**

- What plan does the congregation have in place to express an expectation and afford the pastor an opportunity for life-long learning?

- *Carefully*, discuss with the pastor which strengths and weaknesses would be most strategic for him to address.

- Does the congregation as a whole have a culture of excellence? Explain your observation.

GOING FORWARD:

- Identify one area of concentration for the pastor.

- Identify one area of concentration for the elders or other leadership group.

PRAYER POINTS FOR THE COMING MONTH:

CHAPTER TEN

# IN THE FLESH

Jesus took on flesh. As Christians we should remember we are not Platonists. We are not opposed to the material world. God created it. Sure, man has distorted it, even defaced it, and the material world as a whole is "bent" or "broken." But it is where we live. Like Jesus' incarnation, we live in the material world. We live in the flesh. We live in a world of seeing, hearing, smelling, tasting and touching. The "material" matters and makes an impression. Appearance, sound, aroma, flavor and tactility all make a difference.

Rightly or wrongly, pastors will be judged by their flesh and its "sensation." This section will help you consider how making the most of our "incarnation" can help draw good attention to Jesus, the Incarnate God.

---

## ON SMILING

In your seminary training you learned deep and weighty truths. You studied serious and challenging topics.

This topic might not seem to fit with those categories. But it does. It is a deep and weighty truth. I am serious about it, and it is challenging.

Smile. God really does love you. Really.

Yes, you have a lot going on. Plenty of things fill your day: souls to save, hurts to soothe, sinners to reprove, confirmands to instruct, budgets to balance, sermons to prepare. It is hard work to be a pastor.

*But smile.*

Smiling may be the Church's strongest confession of faith. (It certainly is a lot easier than reciting the Athanasian Creed.)

Look at this word from Habakkuk:

> Though the fig tree does not bud and there are no grapes on the vines, though the olive crop fails and the fields produce no food, though there are no sheep in the pen and no cattle in the stalls, yet I will rejoice in the LORD, I will be joyful in God my Savior. The Sovereign LORD is my strength; he makes my feet like the feet of a deer, he enables me to go on the heights. (Habakkuk 3:17-19)

What a powerful sentiment. With the whole Chaldean army prepared to swoop down and wreak havoc, Habakkuk found something to smile about: God was with him. Joy because of the presence of God, not happiness at what is happening, drives the smile of the child of God.

And he is with you; he *is* present. God is with you to love and care, to forgive and strengthen. *Think on this:* the eternal life-giving God, who made heaven and earth, who has forgiven your sins and promised you all that you need for now and forever, is with you. *That* God *is* with you! So smile.

*Smile, and sometimes laugh, when you preach.* Sure, you proclaim a deep and weighty, serious and challenging message, but at the heart of your proclamation you declare the saving, life-giving presence of God in Christ. In an incarnational way smiling helps the hearers experience the joy of the Gospel.

*Smile, but watch the laughter, when you are comforting the sick or the bereaved.* Here especially a smile serves as a comforting sign of God's presence. Your smile can serve as the incarnation of the Gospel.

*Smile when you are teaching children.* By virtue of your calling, you present a sterner and more imposing figure than you realize. Smiling assures your students that you are also brothers and sisters.

*Smile around your family.* And definitely laugh. Don't let the weight of your office become a burden to them.

*And every once in a while smile in the mirror.* God really does love that goofy person looking back at you.

## ON MANNERS

Please use them.

*You represent the King of Kings.* Mind your manners. Be polite. It is never right to be rude.

Here are a few to keep in mind:

- Take your hat off inside, unless you are a lady, although even ladies should not wear "men's hats" (like ball caps) indoors.
- Be on time for your appointments or call to let the person know that you are delayed.
- Stand up when someone enters the room or approaches a table.
- Do not extend your hand to shake a lady's hand unless she does so first.

- Wash your hands (often).
- Use a tissue or a handkerchief when you sneeze—not your hand or even your elbow.
- Put your napkin in your lap.
- Wait until everyone is served before you begin eating.
- Cut your sandwich in half before you eat it.
- Only cut one bite of meat at a time.
- Don't lick your knife or use it to corral wandering peas.
- No double-dipping.
- Place your knife across the top of your plate when not in use; do not make a bridge with it from the table to your plate.
- Keep one hand in your lap when eating unless it is being used for cutting or holding food.
- Chew with your mouth closed.
- No elbows on the table—it's not a horsey stable! (Remember that from camp?)
- Don't push your plate away from you when you are finished eating.
- Don't call people names or use vulgarities.
- Knock and wait for an invitation to proceed before entering a doorway.
- Wait until the other person has finished speaking before speaking.
- Refrain from using the first name of someone more than a generation older than you until invited.

- Don't point.
- Return phone calls the day you receive them.
- Say "please" and "thank you."
- Don't be the last to leave a party.
- Write thank you notes.
- Don't pass gas of any kind in public.
- Except for your children in private, never correct someone else's manners.

Remember, manners are what separate us from the beasts.

For Further Reading: Judith Martin, "Miss Manners Rescues Western Civilization," or Judith Martin, "The World's Oldest Virtue," "First Things," May 1993.

## ON SHOES

Wear nice ones.

This is especially important for Holy Communion services. When people come forward to receive the Sacrament, they are not quite sure where to look. Many think it is too proud to look up, even if they are looking up to the cross. They won't close their eyes for fear of missing the Sacrament as the celebrant distributes it. This leaves one thing on which to train eyes during the distribution: the pastor's shoes.

And you'll want to make sure they are polished.

Wear nice socks, too. Some day you may be out making a visit, and your host may ask you to remove your shoes, nicely polished as they are.

Nice does not have to be expensive.

I have become friends with some pastors who were trained in Africa. Their training included a course in hygiene. American seminaries might want to think that through. Things like brushed teeth, regular showers, use of deodorant, un-rumpled shirts… and nice, polished shoes will (more than you might realize) lead toward significance and perhaps the saving of souls.

Don't let the length of this post confuse you about its importance. More than shoes are afoot.

## ON CLERICAL GARB

Should pastors wear a robe and a clerical collar? Should they wear khakis and a sport shirt? What about jeans and a tee shirt? Many have spent much time discussing this.

Aren't these kind of funny questions? Of all the issues that we can talk about, how in the world can it matter how a pastor dresses?!?

But it does. Mark Twain said, "Clothes make the man. Naked people have little or no influence on society."

What we wear shapes how people view us. Whether or not that seems superficial, it is the reality. It is also incarnational.

Here is the main principle: we do not want to wear anything that gets in the way of the Gospel message we proclaim. How we look should not impede people's hearing of what we have to say. We are representatives of Jesus, and we want to represent him as well as we can.

### SHIRTS WITH CLERICAL COLLARS

I actually like clerical collar shirts.

They tend to be slimming.

I quit wearing them twenty years ago. It seemed that they got in the way of people hearing what I had to say. Clerical collars put *the wrong kind of distance* between people and me. My habit has become to wear button-down shirts with a tie. A mentor of mine once said, "If you want to be taken seriously, wear a shirt and tie." I do want to be taken seriously, so I do. Always. Well, not during the summer months.

A friend of mine wears a clerical collar shirt every day. He says it is one less decision he has to make in the morning.

Other friends wear sport shirts. For others their uniform dress is jeans and a tee shirt. That strikes me as a little too casual for who we represent and the important work we carry out. But that is not the question.

Here is the question: what message do you want your attire to say about you and the work you do? What you wear will say something. Choose accordingly.

## ROBES FOR WORSHIP

I experimented with not wearing a robe (alb) on Sundays. Again, a number of my friends do not wear them.

It seems to me that a robe on Sunday morning puts *the right kind of distance* between people and me. On Sunday in worship, I do not want them to hear from Dave; I want them to hear from Jesus. Somehow the robe does that. Sure, they know it's me under the robe, but visually the message is that something else, someone else is involved. I wear a robe on Sundays. Always. Well, not during outdoor services in the middle of summer.

Here's what solidified this practice for me. One of our daughters had to be sworn in as a lawyer by a judge. The judge seemed like a nice lady. She was very cheerful and pleasant. But she wore a robe. The robe said something else (the Rule of Law), someone else ("Lady Justice"), was involved. It might seem funny, but the presence of the robe upped the ante of the event. The robe got us to a different place.

That's what a robe can do for the pastor and the congregation on a Sunday morning. We have upped the ante. We are at a different place. We are in the presence of God to hear his message of grace and mercy.

## ONE MORE THING

When I am not working, I dress how I please. Casual. Even a little sloppy sometimes.

In fact, as soon as I get home in the afternoon, even if I have to go back for a meeting in a matter of hours, I change into casual clothes. I want to say to my family (and to me!) Dave/Dad is home. I do not want to be pastor at home, so I dress accordingly.

## SO WHAT TO WEAR...

These are the conclusions I have come to about what to wear. You may come to other conclusions.

As you face the fashions of the day, the customs of the Church and the responsibilities of your Call, focus on the "why" more than the "what." Why you are wearing a particular item of clothing is more important what that particular item of clothing is.

Choosing well is more significant than dressing well.

## Conversation: In the Flesh

BIBLE CONVERSATION:

Read 1 Samuel 16:1-13, especially verse 7. How does this passage support the importance of the four sections just completed?

FOR PERSONAL REFLECTION:

- How would people describe your demeanor? Friendly? Serious? Angry? Smiley?

- Manners can be described as voluntarily limiting your freedom to bring blessing to people around you. List ten specific habits you have that grow out of what you understand to be "good manners."

- You communicate things to people by how you dress. What are you trying to communicate with what you wear? Especially consider what you do or do not wear for worship.

FOR GROUP DISCUSSION:

- A smile goes a long way. Discuss how "smiley" your congregation is. Do people consider it a friendly place? What can you do to make it more so?

- While God does not look on outward appearances, people do. What does the appearance of your congregation's buildings and grounds communicate to the community?

- How are "the fashions of the day" positively or negatively affecting your ministry?

GOING FORWARD:

- Identify one area of concentration for the pastor.
- Identify one area of concentration for the elders or other leadership group.

PRAYER POINTS FOR THE COMING MONTH:

CHAPTER ELEVEN

# LIFE OUT THERE

So much of congregational life focuses, rightly, on the community of the congregation. It is within the context of Christian community that we experience Gospel ministry: Word and Sacraments. The Church and its faith are incurably congregational. It is within the congregation that faith and faithfulness are nourished. It is there we are filled up… so we have something to share "out there"—where the mission is.

The following four topics will help you think about a good connection with life "out there." It certainly influences us "in here" (in the congregation). And we should especially remember that Jesus' last message to his followers before his ascension enjoined them to join him in mission—out there. Ten days later he gave them the power to do so. That same Holy Spirit has been poured out into our lives to connect with life "out there."

## ON MEETING THE NEEDS OF THE COMMUNITY

Much has been written in other places about the importance of the Church and its congregations meeting the needs of the community. Indeed, ministries like coat banks, food pantries, after school youth centers, preschools, recovery groups and so on help meet the needs of the community. What follows is another way to approach *what the community needs from the Church*.

THE COMMUNITY NEEDS US TO READ OUR BIBLE.

While I have previously emphasized the importance of Bible reading for personal spiritual growth (and there is no surer pathway), the *community needs us to read our Bible*. If Christians are going to be witnesses in the community, then we need to be sure witnesses of truth—and that comes from knowing the Word.

THE COMMUNITY NEEDS US TO PRAY—A LOT.

One of the greatest powers that the Church has is its direct access to the throne of Grace. The Church should regularly and aggressively be praying for its community, including:

- Public safety and health workers
- Educators
- The poor and needy

- Government officials

- The unemployed and the underemployed

All of these have special challenges which we can take straight to the God of all creation! Prayer is a work that is essential to do for our community.

### THE COMMUNITY NEEDS US TO TITHE AND MORE.

Generally, people think that tithing is to meet the "needs" of the Church. Not so.

Tithing forces Christians to rely on God instead of being money-oriented. The *community* needs to see Christians trusting in God instead of money. That will give them hope in troubled economic times. They will see there is another way, the way of peace, contentment, calm.

Tithing will keep the Church from acting like merchandisers, non-profits and beggars toward the community. Instead of being *receivers from* the community, we will have *resources to give* to the community.

### THE COMMUNITY NEEDS US TO QUIT TALKING LIKE RUSH LIMBAUGH AND BILL MAHER, HANNITY AND MADOW.

The political conversation and tone in our land is:

- Cynical

- Sarcastic

- Caustic

- Bombastic

It doesn't help the community if the Church speaks with the same kind of voice.

## THE COMMUNITY NEEDS US TO QUIT EXPECTING NON-CHRISTIAN PEOPLE TO BEHAVE BIBLICALLY.

Of course, the Church grieves at the coarse, immoral and unhealthy behavior of so many in our society. But we have to be careful about how we react.

Imagine coming across a terrible automobile accident. If you react with shock and horror at what you see, you will be of little help to the people in need. Rather, you need to be calm and controlled if you really want to be in a position to help. Likewise, the Church should calm down, take a breath, and then gently share with individuals who may be far from Christ that there is a God who loves them right now in spite of their behavior (just as he does us), and that he has a better and more healthy way for life—and help, where relevant, with physical and spiritual needs.

And while we are at it, let's make sure that we turn off all scorn or mockery. It is not funny for Christians to make fun of others. It makes it hard for the community to hear our message of love.

## THE COMMUNITY NEEDS US TO BEHAVE BIBLICALLY.

While we should not expect non-Christians to live like Christians, the community needs to see *us* living as Christians. Jesus saved his harshest words for those who knew better.

As you know, non-Christians in the community have a hard time hearing our message when they see our words not matching our actions. Early Christians were a draw to others because they were distinctively different people.

**THE COMMUNITY NEEDS US TO LOVE ITS CHILDREN.**

Governments can't.
Too many parents are unable or won't.
Jesus does.
So should we.

**THE COMMUNITY NEEDS US TO BE IN PROXIMITY.**

Make sure that you are engaged with neighbors and fellow workers. Coach little league. Participate in a community endeavor. Hang out with friends at a coffee shop. Engage strangers.

Practice *unchurchmanship:* connecting with people *outside of the Church community* to share, through words and deeds, the love of Jesus.

If you want more ideas on this, check out "Just Walk Across the Room" by Bill Hybels.

**THE COMMUNITY NEEDS US TO LOVE ONE ANOTHER IN THE CHURCH.**

Our congregations always need to have reputations of being havens of peace and joy. Unbelievers get confused about discord between believers.

*What the community needs above all things from the Church is for the Church to be the Church.*

---

## ON SPORTS

Nothing besides the Bible may have as big an impact on your ministry as sports. No fooling. We are a sports-crazy nation. You need to study, understand, utilize and be on guard about sports.

## SPORTS AS GOD

Far too often the things of God come in second place to sports. Families choose traveling hockey teams over Sunday morning worship. Church officers choose the Tuesday night basketball game over leadership meetings. Catechism students choose football practice over class. And who can blame them? Sports are far more exciting than church activities.

You might be amazed at what people spend on sports: uniforms, tickets, betting, traveling, fancy recording equipment. And talk about evangelism! No one evangelizes like a sports fan. He is ever ready to share the latest good news about his team.

Be careful. To speak against sports is to be… a spoil sport. And no one likes a spoil sport. Yet if people make sports their god, pastors are compelled to call the thing what it is: idolatry. Be prepared to say so.

You, too. Because of the ubiquitous nature of sports in America, pastors can easily give themselves over to an untoward interest in sports. Be on guard. The difference between an interest and an idol is not great.

## SPORTS AS LITURGY

Liturgy is not dead. It is alive and well and being lived out at a college football game near you. They use vestments with proper liturgical colors: home team, away team, throwback uniforms, band uniforms, refs in black and white, even the ushers have safety green. At certain times the fans stand up and sit down and stand up and sit down. You will hear them singing the same songs week after week; some of these songs have not been changed for decades. Congregants chant pieces of the liturgy over and over: GO GREEN, GO WHITE. Often throughout the game the worshippers share the greeting of peace, "High five it, man." Communion is distributed both in the stands (like Methodists) and in a continuous concession line (like the Catholics)—"*Hot dog here. Get your hot dog!*"

This is not blasphemy; this is necessary. *Study* sports as liturgy. Our Sunday practice of Christian liturgy could be *enhanced* if we learned lessons from sports liturgy: think about the intensity of preparation that precedes a game, watch how the crowd gets geared up for the kick off, consider the high level of involvement of the crowd during the game, don't be leery of using old songs—but do them with gusto! Who knows, if you learn the right lessons from sports liturgy, people may actually be glad when the service goes into overtime. You may be moving toward significance.

### SPORTS AS LINGUA FRANCA

You need to know and follow sports. It is the lingua franca of America. If you are going to communicate with people in America, especially men, you must have a working knowledge of basketball, football, baseball, hockey, golf and NASCAR. You don't have to know all the details, strategies and lingo, but knowing last night's score or the latest standings helps. The further your go into the country the more you need to know about hunting and fishing. In some areas you should know something about MMA. If you are working with younger people, knowledge of X-Games and soccer are helpful.

### SPORTS AS COMMUNITY

Sports teach about human nature and community. You see teamwork. You see hard work. You see high expectations. You see people gathered together cheering and supporting one another. The sporting world has much to teach the Church about life together.

If people are into sports, and if you want to be into people, then you need to be into sports. Sports help conversations get started, "Hey, did you see that game last night?" Sports provide great sermon illustrations. So be a sport. But be careful. Sports are a double-edged sword.

## ON STRAIGHTENING PICTURES

My mother liked straight pictures. When I painted various rooms for her through the years, the worst part of the job was rehanging all the pictures. We had to measure. Mark. Compare the mark to the next picture. Re-measure. Hang. Put the level on it. Take it back down. Re-measure again. Try a new nail over $1/8^{th}$ of an inch. Hang. Move it just a little to the left. No back. Okay, just a bit. There.

About that time someone would shut a door somewhere else in the house, and the picture would move just enough not to be straight. Start over.

She always kept a keen eye on the pictures and hangings throughout the house. Any that got just a little off-kilter would have to be straightened. The ones that habitually moved when doors were closed or people walked by would get just a little tape on the back to keep them in place.

I cannot vouch that every single picture in her house was always absolutely straight, but she sure gave it her best effort.

Pictures should be straight.

She wasn't crazy about crooked pictures outside of her house either. If she was out at a store, she might remark to another how something hanging in the store window wasn't exactly straight. When she visited our house, if I had a picture askew, she would bring it to my attention… gently. At other people's houses I know she noticed when pictures were crooked. She wouldn't talk about it; she would notice it.

Pictures should be straight.

It might not be the end of the world if they are not, but not straight is not straight.

Don't get me wrong about my mother. She was neither neurotic nor rude about this. She understood that there are lots of other issues that need to addressed. She did what she could when she could, but she let the rest of it go. For instance, she would never be so wrapped up in straightening pictures at a funeral home that she would forget to comfort the bereaved.

*Now think theology.*

Theology, like pictures, ought to be straight, orthodox.

As pastor you will, and should, spend much energy making sure that things theological are straight.

But be careful. Be kind. Be polite. Be reasonable.

*Where you have direct responsibility for the theology, be careful.* In your sermons, your Bible classes, your writing, training of other teachers, make sure that you go to great lengths to get things straight. Measure. Re-measure. Correct. Refine.

The theological picture you hang needs to be as straight as you can make it. Take the extra time and effort it takes to get it and keep it straight. Be careful.

*Where you have indirect responsibility for the theology, be kind.* You cannot correct everything that gets said in a Bible class, in a meeting, by an elder, by a staff member. Pick and choose the theology that is most crooked and deal with that. But do it in a kind way. Don't blast fellow members or staff as heretics or fools or know-nothings. Choose your words carefully and make sure your demeanor is friendly.

But do it. It may be your indirect responsibility, but it is your responsibility. Like a mom in a son's home, see what you can do to help keep the pictures straight. But be kind.

*When you have no responsibility for the theological picture, be polite.* You should not butt into the theological affairs of another congregation, even if it is of your own church body, making a fuss over how crooked all the pictures are. There is no gain in being the community's self-appointed theology straightener. Surely you would not take it upon yourself to straighten the pictures at a neighbor's house when you visit.

Yes, theology that is not quite straight is hard to abide. And sure, if a picture was completely falling off the wall at a neighbor's, you would try to catch it. But you are not always positioned to do something about it. There are times when it is really not your business. Be polite.

*When there is something more pressing than the horizontal precision of the theological picture, be reasonable.* Wedding and funeral settings can get a little askew when family members come from all sorts of backgrounds; things can get off-kilter even. When you are working with clergy or congregations of other denominations on social projects in your community, don't plan to fix everyone else's theology when you ought to be driving nails or packing groceries. If you and another Christian from a different theological background are sharing Christ with an unbeliever, don't focus on correcting everything you find off level; focus on sharing Christ.

Sometimes there are fish that need to be fried. Fry the fish. Don't straighten the pictures. Be reasonable.

The church body to which I belong endeavors to get the pictures as straight as possible. We walk around with theological levels at the ready. We love straight pictures.

Sure, pictures ought to be straight. Pictures that aren't straight aren't straight. But we live in an incurably off-kilter world. There is only so much we can do. Be careful. Be kind. Be polite. Be reasonable. A balanced approach to straightening pictures will help on your path toward significance.

## ON PLAYING THE HAND YOU ARE DEALT

The less time you spend trying to be what you are not, and even more so, the less energy you spend forcing your congregation to be what it is not, the better. Don't underestimate the significance of this insight.

God gives some gifts to every person. He does not give all gifts to all people. He has dealt you *some cards but not every card*. In ministry make sure you play the hand you are dealt and not the hand you wish you had. Do not obsess about what cards others in your community or neighboring congregations have.

My family enjoys pinochle. After the dealer deals the cards, each player sorts through the cards and arranges them. The player must assess what can and, even more importantly, what cannot be done in this round given the cards in hand, which tricks likely can be taken and which tricks likely cannot. You cannot play cards you do not have. You must make the most of the cards that you do have.

In ministry God has dealt you certain cards. They include:

- Your personal gifts
- Your family situation
- Your congregation's make-up
- The community's characteristics
- The general tenor of the time

You must sort through these cards and see what the possibilities are and what the limitations are. Nothing is gained trying to have a dynamic college-aged ministry in a community without college students. Do not expect a city congregation to be able to do the ministry that a small-town congregation might do. If you are not particularly gifted in organization and leadership, do not try to grow a mega-church.

Spend time regularly assessing the strength and opportunity of the cards you hold now.

*Play the cards you have, not the ones you wish you had.*

Many congregations and pastors try to be what they cannot become. There is nothing worse than a contemporary service conducted by a congregation that holds the wrong cards for such a service, e.g., a reserved pastor, no contemporary musicians and a reluctant congregation. Congregations in remote locations are better off supporting a city congregation's soup kitchen rather than conducting their own. Some pastors and congregations have the cards to become very large congregations. Others don't.

*Play the cards you have, not the ones you wish you had.*

But play them always as wisely and aggressively as you can. Play hard. Play smart. Remember Paul wrote, "Make the most of every opportunity." (Ephesians 5:16) Also Jesus said, "Whoever can be trusted with very little can also be trusted with much." (Luke 16:10)

If all goes well, your ministry will be a long one. The cards you hold in your hand now are not necessarily the ones you will be dealt in a later round. But you cannot win now with cards you do not have or wish you had or see that someone else has.

Take the tricks now that you can.

*Play the cards you have, not the ones you wish you had.*

Let me give you a special caution regarding books, conferences and seminars designed to help you develop as a pastor and as a congregation. Make sure that you use such resources wisely. Most of these come from a source or a situation that has been holding different cards from what you hold in your hand. Make sure that you think about how to apply these resources based on the reality of what you hold in your hand. If you do not, you will frustrate yourself and confuse your congregation.

*Play the cards you have, not the ones you wish you had.*

I do not know about your psyche; I do know mine. This has been a tough trick for me to stick to through the years. But the less time we worry about the cards we don't have and the more intentional we are about playing well the ones we do have, the more we will move toward significance.

### Conversation: Life Out There

BIBLE CONVERSATION:

Read Acts 17:16-34. How does this passage support the importance of the four issues just covered?

FOR PERSONAL REFLECTION:

- What sort of connections do you have with the community? Do you know community leaders? Do you have a relationship with those involved in sports? Are you connected with community-wide ministries?

- What sort of connections do you have with other clergy from your own denomination? From other denominations? How do you balance supporting your theological position and befriending fellow clergy?

- What are you doing to maintain both contentment in your ministry and urgency in making the most of your opportunities?

FOR GROUP DISCUSSION:

- What does your community know about or think about your congregation? What are you doing to enable your pastor to be connected to the community?

- What can your congregation learn about more effective ministry as it looks at the sports community around it?

- What is your congregation doing to maintain both contentment in its ministry and urgency in making the most of its opportunities?

GOING FORWARD:

- Identify one area of concentration for the pastor.

- Identify one area of concentration for the elders or other leadership group.

PRAYER POINTS FOR THE COMING MONTH:

## CHAPTER TWELVE
# WARNING

There are warning signs for crossing the street. There are warning signs along the highways. There are warning signs on medicine bottles. There are warning signs on children's toys. There are warning signs on clothes. There are warning signs on… warning signs. Well, maybe not.

Pastors are deployed to the front line of the Kingdom's battle. While the victory may be secure, the battle can be brutal and dangerous. The stakes are high. The risks are great. And the opposition is fierce. This is not for the faint of heart. This section will prepare pastors to be properly warned for the battle ahead.

---

### ON JOY

*Never let anyone or anything steal your joy.*

This is significant day in and day out.

You are a child of the Most High God! You have the hosts of heaven helping you and the gates of heaven waiting for you. Your sins, faults and failures are washed clean. God is with you and for you.

Of course, you also have church meetings. And Bible classes to prepare. Deadlines for newsletters loom. You were not where someone else thought you should be. The things you learned at seminary don't seem to answer the questions you now have. This is hard work.

*Never let anyone or anything steal your joy.*

There are things that need to be taken care of at home. There are things that need to be taken care of in the office. There are things that need to be taken care of in the world. Oh, the things there are!

*Never let anyone or anything steal your joy.*

You will get tired. You will get confused. You will get hurt. You will get tested and tempted.

*Never let anyone or anything steal your joy.*

Without joy you cannot carry on—for long. Without joy you will become dry, brittle and bitter. Without joy you will become a bane instead of a blessing to your family and congregation.

Where then joy? In Jesus!

Remember joy is different than happiness. Happiness is based on… what happens. Joy is centered in the grace and love God has for you in Jesus.

I always liked the book of Habakkuk, and I know this is the second time I have quoted it in this book. I can remember a seminary professor quoting it in Hebrew. I did not understand it in Hebrew; I treasure it in English! Habakkuk found joy in the presence, nature and promise of God.

> Though the fig tree does not bud and there are no grapes on the vines, though the olive crop fails and the fields produce no food, though there are no sheep in the pen and no cattle in the stalls, yet I will rejoice in the LORD, I will be joyful in God

my Savior. The Sovereign LORD is my strength; he makes my feet like the feet of a deer, he enables me to go on the heights. Habakkuk 3:17-19

*Never let anyone or anything steal your joy.*
Keep your eyes fixed on Jesus; the hope he gives will lead you toward significant joy.

---

## ON DISCOURAGEMENT

*Discouragement is a demon.*

In *This Present Darkness* Frank Peretti gave a great picture of demonic oppression. He personalized how certain demons plague the people of God. The idea was revelatory. I do not suppose that he was all right. But he certainly was not all wrong.

*Discouragement is a demon.*

It sits on your shoulder. It bores into your brain. It steals your energy.

At least three staff issues need to be addressed in my congregation. I have addressed none of them well. During the past week two somewhat glaring mistakes I would have caught if I had proofread more carefully got out into public. While they were relatively small items in the scheme of things, they were the worst kind of mistakes: unnecessary. One of the books I am reading makes me wonder if about half of what I have going on in the congregation is in error. Add these: the couple I am counseling whose marriage is getting no better, the catechism students who seem oblivious to the import of what we are doing, the adults in the congregation who behave like children. And to top it all off, I got too great of a dose of talk radio this week.

Depressed? No.

But discouraged.

Of course, discouragement means "loss of heart."

Expect it.

As a pastor expect there to be times when one of Satan's demons strikes at the core of your courage. Just when you need energy, conviction and joy to move forward on something, you will meet discouragement.

Meet it. But do not give in to it. Understand it to be what it is: a stinking gift from the bowels of hell. Return it to the hellish fiend who sent it *unopened*. Mark it: *return to sender*.

Dwelling in discouragement is one of the more disastrous things a pastor can do. It can develop into substance abuse, family disruption, binge spending and generally grouchy Christianity.

First Samuel 7:12-14 talks about an Ebenezer Stone. It is a stone of remembrance designed to forestall discouragement. Take a quick moment to read about it.

Because you can anticipate times of discouragement to come, place certain "Ebenezer Stones" in your mind and your life. Along with the passage from Habakkuk cited previously, a second passage that serves to strengthen my heart and shore up my courage as an Ebenezer Stone comes from the book of Joshua.

> As I was with Moses, so I will be with you; I will never leave you nor forsake you. Be strong and courageous. (Joshua 1:5-6)

Discouraged?

Yes, now and then. But never for long! "Greater is he who is in you than he who is in the world." (1 John 4:4) Jesus' love restores our heart and keeps our feet firm on the path toward significance.

## ON BOUNDARIES

The following will get you out of trouble before you get into it.

Robert Frost remarked wisely, "Good fences make good neighbors." Proverbs 23:10 warns against moving ancient boundary stones. In "Dare to Discipline" James Dobson writes about the importance of boundary-setting for raising children.

*Make sure that you have appropriate and firm boundaries in place.* You will be a much better neighbor, husband and pastor if you do. Figure out now, in advance of situations, how far you will go or not go in any particular area. Now, while you are not in the heat of passion, what makes sense to put off limits? This will keep you from getting knocked off the path toward significance.

Consider boundaries especially in the following areas.

### TOUCH BOUNDARIES

Who will you touch? How will you touch them? Where will you touch them?

Touch is powerful. Touch is incarnational. Touch is therapeutic.

But it can also get you into a lot of trouble. Dangerous touch can lead to bad touch which can lead to disastrous touch. Touch can easily be misconstrued by you, the person you touch or the person who sees you touch the person you touch.

Make sure you have touch boundaries.

- *Be especially careful with women.* It is better by far to be perceived as somewhat aloof than to be perceived as "too huggie." A warm handshake is "touch enough" for almost every situation between men and women, and even then, a gentleman should wait for the lady to extend her hand. Over time there may be friendships that you and your wife make with other couples that will lead to a mutual hug. Take the lead from your wife about which couples that might be. Feel free to hug ladies seventy-five years and older—but be prepared to explain to your wife where the red lipstick on your cheek came from. In this area the general boundary is that less is more.

- *Be especially careful with children.* Children thrive on touch. It is important for pastors to touch children appropriately. Place your hand on their heads during a Communion blessing. Shake their hands when you greet their parents, even stooping to their eye level. Touch a shoulder of an unruly young man in a catechism class. It is unwise to touch a child when no one else is around. Never touch a child in any way that may be misconstrued by a casual observer.

Any touch that seems the least bit inappropriate is. Back off. You are out of bounds.

### TIME BOUNDARIES

Be careful how you apportion your time. Benjamin Franklin said, "Dost thou love life? Then do not squander time, for that's the stuff life is made of." Predetermined boundaries are crucial for time, and thus life management. Make sure that you have boundaries in place for the following:

- *Home Bound Visits*: Most of those you visit as home bound members would love for you to spend an afternoon. That's a nice idea, but you have lots of other things that need attention. My boundary is thirty to forty-five minutes.

- *Hospital Visits*: Most of those you visit *DO NOT* want you to spend an afternoon. They are sick. They need rest. My boundary is ten to fifteen minutes.

- *Sermon Prep*: At the seminary they teach that we should spend eight or more hours a week on sermon preparation. For the life of me I have never known where I would find that kind of time or what I would do with it! My boundary is six to seven hours.

- *Work Week*: Yours is not a forty-hours a week job. But neither should it be an eighty-hours a week job. If you are working only forty hours a week, you are cheating your congregation. If you are working eighty hours a week, you are cheating your family and not really helping your congregation. My boundary is fifty to fifty-five hours.

- *Counseling Sessions*: You need to set boundaries both in regard to how long a session will be and how many sessions you will have with an individual or couple. My boundary is an hour. (Keep a clock unobtrusively visible.) My other boundary is three. If I can't help someone in three visits, it is time to make a referral to a counselor.

- *Meetings*: Somewhere I heard that nothing good happens in a church meeting after 45 minutes. I believe it but seldom can pull it off. My boundary is ninety minutes.

TALKING BOUNDARIES

Take heed to what your mother must have said to you at some point,

"Watch your mouth."

Pastors talk. Pastors talk a lot.

Sometimes pastors can talk too much. Or talk too much about things they shouldn't.

- *Make sure you do not fall into the habit of having to comment on everything someone else says just because you are the pastor.* I confess that at meetings I fall into the habit of always having to contribute something to everything that gets said, even if it is just a humorous comment. I have to intentionally set a boundary relative to how often I will speak up.

- *Determine what words are off limits to you.* Too often I hear brother pastors use "salty language" in an attempt to be "real." Nope. Those words that tend to have four letters and that describe body parts or body functions ought to be outside our boundaries.

- *Strictly limit how much you talk about your family. Strictly!* Talking a lot about your family is not fair to them and not nearly as interesting to others as you think it is.

- *Never betray a confidence.* If you are not sure if something was said in confidence, assume it was.

- *Don't go negative.* We live in a put-down culture. Some comics have gotten rich perfecting the art of the put-down. If what you have to say does not build up, it is out of bounds.

Manage your boundaries, and you should manage to stay out of trouble. You will also find yourself far more productive and at peace.

NOTE: A pastor friend who read an advance copy of this book suggested the following about this section. "You might put this whole essay in bold and about size 36 font. The issue of boundaries is one of the greatest reasons otherwise good men go down."

## ON WAR

Make no mistake, you are at war. Make no mistake.

Don't let the friendly narthex post-worship chit chat, the tedious evening elders' meeting or the youth bowling event fool you. You are at war.

Satan and his hounds of hell hate what you are doing and the One you serve. They exert their eternal energies to discourage, disrupt and destroy you, your family and your congregation.

Pastoral ministry is not for faint hearts or squeamish stomachs.

Before you go any further here, read Ephesians 6:10-20. Go on. Read it.

### TRAINING

Soldiers must commit themselves to a life of training. Soldiers' training *begins* in basic training. That's why it's called "basic training." The initial training for soldiers only gets them started. They must continue throughout their time of service to train for battle. They must work to keep in shape. Learn new techniques for battles and practice old ones. They must study the history of war. They must study emerging enemy tactics.

Commit yourself to being trained and training others. Be hard on others; be harder on yourself. You are at war.

- Spiritual training is a must. Bible reading above all, relentless prayer, fasting, tithing (this forestalls divided loyalties), solitude, celebration, et al.

- Physical training counts too. Do not underestimate the physical challenges of spiritual warfare. Make sure that you address the Big Four: exercise, diet, alcohol and sleep.

## COMRADES

Only fools fight alone. Build strategic relationships with other soldiers in the Lord's army.

As pastor you have a responsibility to build harmony and concord with and within your congregation. Internal skirmishes in a congregation and between a congregation and pastor eviscerate the fighting force.

View your denomination as a strategic alliance. Look to the national church body for more than a pension. See it as a supply chain. See the local and regional groupings of your church body as ways to bring order to the battle. See older pastors as seasoned veterans. See younger pastors as freshly minted officers who need mentoring.

Consider other local Christian congregations as comrades. Take this crucial step in spiritual warfare. Like allies in World War II you can maintain your "spiritual nationality" and still fight a common enemy. Lutherans don't have to become Baptists to appreciate that Baptists too are in the community for Jesus. Nor is it necessary for Baptists to "cure" Lutherans of being Lutheran before they both join in battle. Americans did not become Brits nor did Brits become Americans to wage battle against the Nazis. If the local Christian congregation is taking it to the enemy in one area of ministry, celebrate that, do not compete with it, and then find your own battle front. Spiritual warfare becomes more significant when local clergy can coordinate in a community battle plan.

## BOREDOM

War, like football, is characterized by lots of inaction. In a sixty-minute football game the ball is in play only about eleven to twelve minutes. War is like that too. There is a lot more sitting, waiting, thinking than there is actual action.

Football players and warriors must fight boredom and stay vigilant.

Think about that Thursday night in the garden with the looming Good Friday battle. Where do we find the most famous soldiers in all Church history? Sleeping, nodding, dozing.

Jesus enjoined them to watch and pray.

So much of what a pastor does is routine. So little of what a pastor does seems to actually move the ball down the field.

Beware boredom. Be vigilant. Watch. Pray. This is no game; you are at war.

### COURAGE

They say dogs smell fear. When passing by a snarling dog, you don't want him to know you are scared.

Courage, man!

Satan is no dog; he is a prowling lion seeking whom he may devour.

Courage, man!

Think of words associated with "pastor." What words come to mind? Faithful? Kind? Knowledgeable? Loving? Should "courageous" come to mind?

If you are going to make it in pastoral ministry, you'd better focus on this word: courage.

### CONFIDENCE

Confidence gives rise to courage.

Find courage through confidence in God.

Remember: greater is he who is in you than he who is in the world.

(1 John 4:4)

Remember: the one who created the heavens and the earth promises that nothing can snatch us out of his hands. (John 10:29)

Remember: you do not need to fear the one who only has power to kill the body and nothing more. (Matthew 10:28)

Remember: in Christ you are already more than a conqueror through faith in Christ Jesus. (Romans 8:37)

And so… into battle. Make no mistake: you are at war, and the stakes are significant.

### Conversation: Warning

BIBLE CONVERSATION:

Read Ephesians 6:1-20. How does this passage support the importance of the four topics just completed?

FOR PERSONAL REFLECTION:

- What can you do to nurture and maintain joy while forestalling discouragement?

- What boundaries have you placed in your life to help maintain a ministry of significance? What new ones might you implement?

- What alliances have you built to help you in the battle of the Kingdom?

**FOR GROUP DISCUSSION:**

- What are you doing as leaders to cultivate a spirit of joy in your congregation?

- What boundaries does your congregation have in place to protect the congregation's ministry? What new ones might you implement?

- How is your congregation building alliances with others in the Christian community?

**GOING FORWARD:**

- Identify one area of concentration for the pastor.

- Identify one area of concentration for the elders or other leadership group.

**PRAYER POINTS FOR THE COMING MONTH:**

CHAPTER THIRTEEN

# EMBRACE THE ADVENTURE

Significant ministry calls for adventure. Significant ministry consists in pilgrimage. I always liked Psalm 84:5, especially how it reads in the NIV. "Blessed are those whose strength is in you, whose hearts are set on *pilgrimage*." Pilgrimage. We are not home yet. We are now already with him, Jesus, but not yet home. The life of the Christian generally, and the life of a pastor specifically, is thus an adventure. Like hiking the Kaibab Trail into the Grand Canyon, some stretches are arduous, some stretches are a piece of cake, but the entire experience is a great adventure.

The final topics invite you to embrace with both arms and with all your heart the adventure of being a pastor. Certainty. Uncertainty. Darkness. Light. Learning. Teaching. Following. Leading. Receiving. Giving. Life. Death. Life Again. And in all circumstances, Thanking.

## ON JUGGLING

If you are going to serve as a pastor, you'd better learn to juggle.

You have multiple responsibilities: child of God, husband, father, son, pastor, community member, churchman.

As a pastor you have multiple tasks:

- Preaching
- Leading
- Worship planning
- Strategic planning
- Financial planning
- Teaching adults
- Teaching young people
- Teaching children (these three teaching responsibilities are dramatically different)
- Grief counseling
- Pre-marriage and marriage counseling
- End of life counseling
- "Bossing"
- "Scholaring"
- Occasional plumbing
- Lawn mowing and snow shoveling—sometimes

- And so on…

Being a pastor is more like being a homemaker than any other job. Homemakers too have a wide variety of responsibilities.

You will never get it all right all of the time. It helps to do the following:

- List your priorities and loyalties in order. (Remember, God and the congregation are not synonymous.)
- List your goals. Goals should include personal, family and professional goals.
- Make sure that both of these lists are consistent with the Word of God and your gift mix. Also make sure that these are consistent with your confidence that you will live forever *in heaven* and *do not need to create it here*!
- Add as few extraneous activities and hobbies as possible.

It is hard to balance all that you need to do. To date, I have not found that it is at any time not hard.

One Thursday one of my members asked me to come out to an event Saturday morning at 8:00 a.m. to lead an opening prayer for a community building project. He thought it was important to have the pastor present—just for a prayer. I declined explaining that my morning was already full. It is not that I am not an early riser on Saturdays. I did some Bible reading at 5:00 a.m. Plus, I had to drop a daughter off at a sporting event at 6:00 a.m. I wanted to get a half hour on the treadmill done as well.

With all that, I still really had plenty of time if I hurried to run over and do what he requested.

I made Saturday morning breakfast for my wife instead.

Here's how I juggled things: I needed to start the day with the Word. That came first. Also, I needed to make sure that I cared for my family. So it came second—a ride for my daughter and breakfast for my wife. Third, I must care for my body so I chose to get a run done before I got too far into the day. Fourth, I needed to teach that new member class because that is something that pastors are specially trained to do.

Praying at a community building project would have been nice. Probably it would have been good exposure. It clearly was possible. But I figured:

- Someone else could do it just as well as I. It would have been nice, but surely not necessary.

- My motivation for going would have been more self-serving than anything—if I had gone it would have been so that this member who asked me to do something was not ticked off at me.

- It may have taught people the wrong thing: prayers only matter if the pastor does them.

- There are enough other times that I have to choose to let one of the other priorities (walk with God, care for family, care for self) come in second—at least for a time. This was not a crucial time to do that for the preceding three reasons.

So that day, I let that ball drop. Someone else said a prayer.

You can take this to the bank: you cannot juggle all of the balls that you and others would like juggled all at the same time all the time. You *MUST* let some drop. Choose wisely, prayerfully, honestly. Your choosing will impede or speed your path toward significance.

A friend from church sent this. It should help.

"Imagine life is a game in which you are juggling five

balls. The balls are called work, family, health, friends, and integrity. You're keeping all of them in the air. But one day you finally come to understand that work is a rubber ball. If you drop it, it will bounce back. The other four balls—family, health, friends, integrity—are made of glass. If you drop one of these, it will be irrevocably scuffed, nicked, perhaps even shattered. And once you truly understand the lesson of the five balls, you will have the beginnings of balance in your life."

*Suzanne's Diary for Nicholas*, James Patterson

God bless the juggling, a significant part of the adventure.

---

## ON TINKERING

Pastoral ministry is an inexact science. It calls for experimentation. It calls for artfulness. It calls for tinkering.

*Plan to tinker.*

One of the biggest surprises to me in the pastoral ministry was that there is no clear path on how everything really should be done and how everything really fits together or how everything really works.

After nearly four decades of ministry, there continue to be nights when I come home convinced I have no idea of what I am doing or what I should be doing.

Not that there isn't a lot of help!

Those pastors who have had "successful" significant ministries write books and lead seminars. Business leaders have articles one can read and conferences one can attend. Hopefully, much of what your professors at seminary said still echoes in your head. You have laypeople who have both strong and helpful advice. (Sometimes their strong advice is not helpful, and some of their helpful advice is not strong.)

How do you put it all together for significance in ministry?

And then there is the situation on the ground. The real-life situation in which you minister often differs from situations that others address. Others may speak to a different time, a different place, a different culture. They may speak from a different theological position, with different constraints, for different ends.

How do you synthesize all that everyone else is saying, doing, teaching with the circumstances, frustrations, opportunities, assets and liabilities that you have?

*Plan to tinker.*

A ministry based on tinkering allows for four dynamics.

Tinkering necessitates patience. Picture a granddad out in a garage with some tools, some other gadgets, a couple of whatchamacallits, some wood and wire, a problem to solve and some decent ideas. He experiments. It doesn't work. He tries something else. That isn't quite right either. He sets it aside until later in the week. Sleeps on it. He comes back to the problem off and on for a couple of weeks, and finally, there it is! It works: an automatic rake that rakes, piles and bags leaves all at once.

Don't try to get everything all figured out at the front end of your ministry. It doesn't work that way. Be patient. Tinker. Try this. Try that. Come back to it later. Tinkering necessitates and breeds patience. (Wasn't your granddad one of the most patient people you knew?)

*Patience is a crucial tool for ministry.*

Tinkering thrives on playfulness. Whimsy. New approaches. Different connections. "Hey, what if I put this and that and that other thing together? I wonder what that would look like?" "This would never fit with that, but I think I will try it." Remember, most of the best things you learned as a child grew out of play time. For you to tinker, you will need a wry smile, a silly notion, a cockamamie idea. This is *NOT* a call for irreverence (see Chapter Two); it is a call for playfulness.

*Playfulness is a crucial tool for ministry.*

Tinkering provides freedom for a fresh start. You may tinker with something for months and no matter what you do, you can't make it work. So, you set it aside. Put it up on the shelf and leave it until later. In the meantime, you begin to tinker on something else.

Too often in ministry we get locked into something that, no matter how hard we and others try, just never seems to work. If you have a "tinker mentality," you will feel free to set it aside, put it up on the shelf and leave it until later. In the meantime, you can move on to something else. Time is too short, and resources are too few, to get locked into things in ministry that aren't working. If you lessen your emotional investment (the word "tinker" connotes limited investment), you will be more likely to move on to the next idea.

*Freedom for a fresh start is a crucial tool for ministry.*

Tinkering allows for serendipity. The word "serendipity" comes from a Persian tale of three princes from Serindip who by accident and happenstance determine the nature of a lost camel. Put enough incongruent things together, and no telling what might happen.

You have experienced serendipity. A movie you watched happened to give you an insight into a counseling situation that made you think of a Bible passage that led you to an insight for a sermon that helped to change a person's life. You did not sit down to watch a movie so that you could change a life. It worked out that way. It is called serendipity. Or in our parlance, it is called the hand of God. Serendipity allows room for God!

*Serendipity is a crucial tool for ministry.*

So, don't get too anxious about what isn't working. Don't get too focused in any one direction. Books, conferences, articles, sage advice: put some of this together with some of that.

*Tinker.*

See where God leads. Pastoral ministry is an inexact science. The adventurous pastor who tinkers is the pastor who is on the path toward significance.

## ON YOUR PASTORAL EXAMPLE

You will teach much with words. You may teach more with your example, how you live.

Or at least your teaching with words will be buttressed or hamstrung by your example. Do not underestimate the influence of example. Remember, after many years of God's proclamation to his people through the words of the prophets, he showed more clearly and completely the center of his message through the Incarnation of the Word. Ultimately, it was actions congruent with words that unleashed the power of the Church: Jesus was God's living demonstration of the Gospel message declared by his prophets.

You, to a lesser degree, are too. You are an incarnation of God's Gospel message. Your actions will make your words all the more significant. There are two ways you should concentrate on your pastoral example.

### CONGRUENCY OF WORDS AND DEEDS

You must avoid endangering your congregation (or family!) with cognitive dissonance. If they hear you saying one thing and see you doing another, they will have a difficult time following your lead. Your words and deeds must match. Consider these areas:

- If you call your people to grow in prayer, giving, helping, reading, serving, forgiving, but do not do so yourself, they will soon learn that those things are not important after all.

- If you are critical, sarcastic or cutting toward others, no matter how much you call people to love and forgive, you will probably grow a conflicted congregation.

- If you are friendly, engaging people both young and old in the narthex before worship, you will most likely develop a warm worship setting without having to talk about it from the chancel.

- Your people will learn more about how to love their families from how you treat your family than by listening to what you say from the pulpit. Conversely, your family will learn more about God's love by seeing how you treat your flock than by what you say at family devotions.

This is simple and obvious but crucial: to be an effective pastor making a significant impact on others, your words and deeds must be congruent. You must demonstrate what you mean by how you live.

Here's where it gets scary. Your words will not always match your deeds. After all, you are still a poor miserable sinner! No matter how hard you try to hide them, you will have character traits and actions that you would prefer are not imitated by your congregation. How you are *IS* how your congregation will become.

Let me say that again. How you are *IS* how your congregation will become. The flock will be molded in the image of the shepherd. You will see your sanctification success lived out by your people, but you will see your sanctification failure lived out as well.

How's that for scary?

That leads to the second point, which is no excuse for not working harder on the first point.

## ORIENTATION OF LIFE AND HOPE

The most powerful example you can give to your people is to be an example of Hebrews 12:2. "Let us fix our eyes on Jesus, the author and perfecter of our faith."

Picture a crowded, busy street full of pedestrians. Suddenly, without saying a word, one of the pedestrians stops and looks toward the sky. A passerby notices and cranes his head heavenward too. "What is up there?" A second does it as well. Then pretty soon another and another stops and looks up. You can predict what happens. Soon the whole street full of people is looking up.

Get it?

When others see the eyes of your faith trained on Jesus, they too will be drawn to look heavenward. First one, then another, and pretty soon the whole congregation will be following your example by having eyes fixed on Jesus. When your life and hope are clearly oriented toward the love God has for you in Jesus, you will be providing an example that trumps every other example you set. And, without that example, no other example will suffice.

Make sure your congregation, its leaders, its staff, its children, its new-comers and long-timers see you with your eyes fixed on Jesus; set that example above all others.

And when you do that, your pastorate will be one of significance: eternal. Now that's an adventure.

## ON PASTORAL PERSPECTIVE

In pastoral ministry, keeping perspective is significant for a ministry of significance.

### REMEMBER, IT IS A JOB.

Being a pastor is your job. It is hard work. You will need to work hard; you will need to work smart. Never apologize for being paid to do this work.

Jesus is the Good Shepherd. You are not. You are, in a very real sense, a hireling. This does not mean you can ever abuse or neglect the flock. It does mean that there are nights that you should go home, crack open a beer and forget about the congregation and its issues. Let Jesus worry. It's his flock.

It is a job. Get up in the morning and go do it. Come home in the evening and let it go.

### REMEMBER, IT IS A PROFESSION.

Have you heard this: the difference between a job and a profession is about fifteen hours a week?

You need to think about being a pastor as also having a profession. You cannot go home, crack open a beer and forget about the congregation and its issues every night, at least not always at 5:30.

There are two other characteristics of the three historic professions, medicine, law and theology, which you must honor. These were mentioned in Chapter Eight but bear repeating.

First, you must exercise confidentiality. People bare their souls to you. You know intimate details about people and their families. Such details can burden you. But such details must remain with you. Keeping a confidence is a professional duty.

Second, you must continue to learn. If you expect the local computer technician to stay current and informed, how much more should you expect your doctor and attorney to be well read and current? And of all the things that help people, computer technology, medicine and the law, nothing is more crucial for helping people than theology, God's Word.

You are a professional. Read. Study. Learn.

Note: Historically high pay was not characteristic of professions. Only in the last few decades has the word professional become connected with money. We now use the word to contrast the difference between someone who "does it for money" and someone who "does it without pay," i.e., professional dish washer or professional mechanic. We also assume that at least some of the historic professions, i.e. doctors and lawyers will be highly paid. Do not expect that you being a professional will translate into a high salary. (This too was mentioned in Chapter Eight and likewise bears repeating.)

REMEMBER, IT IS A CALLING.

Go to a local high school band, orchestra or choir concert. You will be impressed by the conductor.

Follow a local high school sports team. Get to know a tennis or cross country or swimming program. You will be impressed by the coach.

Most conductors and coaches can't give you a logical reason for doing what they do. The hours are long and crazy. The frustrations are many. The financial benefits are not what they would reap if they devoted the same time and energy to some other endeavor. Balancing their efforts with family and other interests is a challenge.

But there they are. There they serve. There they make a significant difference in the lives of others.

They may have tried to quit at different times, but somehow, they just couldn't.

They have the right gift mix, inclination and unquenchable love for the field (music, sports). They are called. Called. It is how God has made them to participate in his larger community.

Your work as a pastor is a calling, a *Calling*.

You are to do it not for yourself. Sure you will derive your living from the work (it's a job), and, yes, you will experience self-improvement on your path to greater effectiveness (a profession), but being a pastor is much bigger than you. You are Called. It is how God has made you to participate in his larger community.

Now this realization may not be evident at the start. Even though our church's practice is to identify called pastors as those certified seminary graduates who have a Call from a congregation, at some point you will also experience a "sense of Calling."

I did not have it before becoming a pastor. I did not have it when I became a pastor. For me it hit at about the fifteen-year mark. It was then that I realized being a pastor is what I am wired to do, it is what God has equipped me to do, it is what God wants me to do. Try as I might, I could not quit. God had a Call on my life.

As you serve as a pastor, look for Calling.

There may come a time when you become convinced you are not really equipped or designed for being a pastor, that it is not your Calling. Go find something else to do—a different job or profession. Search out what your Calling is. You will burn out from the hard work of being a pastor if it is not your Calling.

I hope for you a point of great clarity, a time when you become convinced being a pastor really is your Calling, far more than a job or a profession. You will have hit the sweet spot. The Biblical word for that is *blessed*.

Dig in.

## REMEMBER, IT IS A GIFT.

I have had a number of people, intending to encourage me, who have said, "Pastor, I wouldn't want your job!"

There are days you won't want it either. There are days you will envy the Walmart greeter.

Remember, being a pastor is also a gift from God. This is not your choosing. He has chosen, even Called you to do this. Your pastorate is a gift from God to you.

You should always do two things with any gift you receive: be grateful for it and fruitful with it.

Give thanks to God for the gift of being a pastor. Gratitude must completely trump any sense of pride. "Thank you, God, for giving me the chance to serve in this way."

Be fruitful. The "gift of the pastorate" is not like the gift of a tie or socks from a preschool student. You don't stuff this gift in a bottom drawer. It is a gift *from God*. Always seek the best and highest use of the gift God has given you.

And no grousing. God gives nothing but good gifts!

So, pastor, enjoy the adventure…. work hard, learn lots, serve lovingly, shine your shoes, give thanks.

And show them Jesus. Always. He must increase. You must decrease.

That's the path toward significance.

## Conversation: Embrace the Adventure

**BIBLE CONVERSATION:**

Read Psalm 1. How does this passage support the importance of the four final topics?

**FOR PERSONAL REFLECTION:**

- How are you doing "keeping all the balls in the air?" What does your family think about your "juggling act?" What does your congregation think about it?

- How is your congregation becoming more like you? What do you wish it was that it is not, and how might you shape it?

- Why are you a pastor?

**FOR GROUP DISCUSSION:**

- How are you giving your pastor the freedom to tinker?

- What impact has your pastor had on your life through his example?

- What more can you do to encourage and support your pastor in his Calling?

GOING FORWARD:

- Identify one area of concentration for the pastor.

- Identify one area of concentration for the elders or other leadership group.

PRAYER POINTS FOR THE COMING MONTH:

## ADDITIONAL RESOURCES

### BOOK SALES

For more purchasing options and information on the book, visit the publisher at www.tenthpowerpublishing.com. For quantity discounts when purchasing copies for your board, contact the author directly.

### CONSULTING

Rev. David A. Davis regularly writes fresh content online at his website to guide leaders, pastors, non-profits and congregations toward significance.

In addition, to help you or your organization make the most of the opportunities that God has given you on a path toward significance, the author is available to discuss any of the following topics:

- Development of retreats and conferences that make a lasting difference
- Maximizing opportunities for congregations with average worship size of 250-800
- Tips and insights for significant pastoral impact
- Tips and insights for young Christian leaders
- Best practices for meetings
- Effective use of Policy-Based Governance for congregations and non-profits

Contact the author for more information at his website.

www.towardsignificance.com

www.ingramcontent.com/pod-product-compliance
Lightning Source LLC
Chambersburg PA
CBHW060524100426
42743CB00009B/1428